D0760624

Exceptional Parent Magazine
555 Kinderkamack Road
Oradell, NJ 07649

ISBN: 0-930958-01-2

U.S. $19.95

NO APOLOGIES FOR RITALIN

Vidya Bhushan Gupta, MD

To My Patients

Preface

Bookstore shelves are full of an ever-increasing number of books about attention deficit disorder (ADD). Many of these books take a partisan position for or against Ritalin. The books against Ritalin build their case through a few anecdotes and go on to propose their own brand of treatment—often based upon pseudoscience—exhorting parents to ignore scientific skepticism and follow their advice. Others argue that Ritalin is evil simply because its use has become so rampant, so rapidly. Whereas the authors of anti-Ritalin books are unabashed in their criticisms, despite little scientific evidence to support their claims, the authors of pro-Ritalin books are defensive about recommending it, despite 300-plus scientific studies that have shown that it is safe and effective in ADD.

The controversy surrounding treatment, whether Ritalin or otherwise, is inherent in the nature of behavioral disorders as a whole because most occur along a spectrum ranging from an unequivocally sick state to an unequivocally normal state, leaving a no man's land in between where one cannot say with certainty whether one is sick or normal. Their cause is neither in the body nor in the mind, but in both, and, additionally, in the environment. Their clinical picture is variable, defying definition by diagnostic labels. Similarly, their treatment is not amenable to a cookbook approach, but is eclectic or multimodal, drawing upon many sources, both chemical and therapeutic. Ritalin and related medications are, perhaps, the most important in this multimodal array of treatments available for treating ADD. Although the use of Ritalin in the United States has increased dramatically in the last two decades and should be looked into to ensure proper use, this does not invalidate Ritalin as an effective medication for ADD.

This book is an attempt to educate parents of children with ADD about various treatments available to treat it, so that they can make informed choices. In it, I have used the term "attention deficit disorder" (ADD) rather than "attention deficit hyperactivity disorder" (ADHD) to highlight the primacy of attention deficit over hyperactivity in this condition.

In the first half of this book, I have described what is medically known about this condition: what ADD is, what causes it, and how it is diagnosed. In the second half, I have presented various treatment options: conventional, such as,

Ritalin and related medications; alternative, such as, diets, herbs, and biofeedback; and supportive, such as, psychotherapy and behavior modification. I have discussed the controversy surrounding the use of Ritalin and tried to dispel myths surrounding ADD and Ritalin: "ADD is not a disease; it is simply a difference of temperament"; "ADD is due to poor parenting"; "Ritalin is a mind-altering drug like speed"; "Don't give Ritalin to your children, because they get hooked on it." I have further explored pros and cons of alternative and supportive treatments. I have also tried to caution parents about charlatans, the purveyors of snake oil, who make extravagant claims based upon testimonials, to cash in on parents' frustrations. I offer a framework for parents to evaluate the merits of any treatment, according to generally accepted principles of logic and to information available in the scientific literature.

Although this book has a professional slant, as do most books on this topic, I do not take a partisan position regarding Ritalin. Nor am I apologetic about it.

I hope that, after reading this book, parents of children with ADD will not blame themselves for their child's predicament and will be able to use all the available treatments, including Ritalin, without guilt.

I wish to thank my son, Pranav Gupta, for his help at all stages of this endeavor. Thanks are also due to Diane Khoury, who gave me editorial suggestions; to Aaron Elson, who guided me in formatting the text; Hilda Barry, for her encouragement; and to Carlos Montorfano, MD, for his pithy critique.

Vidya Bhushan Gupta, MD, MPH, FAAP
Demarest, New Jersey

Table of Contents

Section I

THE ESSENCE OF ADD

". . for she was one of those busy, tripping creatures, that can be no more contained in one place than a sunbeam or a summer breeze,"

HARRIET BEECHER STOWE, *Uncle Tom's Cabin*

1

Is ADD Real or a Figment of the Imagination?

SHAWN

Shawn, a six-and-a-half-year-old African-American child, is brought to the behavioral pediatrics clinic of a city hospital in East Harlem by his 55-year-old foster mother, a visibly harried, heavy-set African-American woman. The nurse greets Shawn with a routine "Hi," but he, unmindful of her greeting, walks to the computer at the nursing station, frantically taps its keys, and returns to pull at the stethoscope hanging around her neck. She is hurt and shocked and quickly escorts him to the pediatrician's office where, within five seconds, he touches the garbage can, the container for discarding used needles, and the blood pressure instrument. He then goes under the pediatrician's chair to look into the pediatrician's filing cabinet. He continues to do this despite many requests to sit down and play with the dollhouse or to draw something on a piece of paper. He smiles impishly, without any awareness of the havoc he is wreaking, his large, pretty eyes and cute demeanor disguising his turbulent mind. His foster mother—actually his maternal grandmother—slumps in a chair, breathing heavily, almost wheezing, and starts rattling off her tale of woe.

"He cannot stay still," she says. "He is always on the go, running all over the house, turning the television on and off, and opening and closing the refrigerator. He goes to bed at 11 P.M. and does not fall asleep until 12 midnight. And Lord have mercy! He tosses and turns in the bed while sleeping at night. Look at them notes from the school."

She pulls out a wad of crumpled papers from her pocketbook—notes from Shawn's school—and lays them on the pediatrician's desk. The teacher repeatedly reports that Shawn does not sit quietly in the classroom, forgets instructions, disturbs other children, and constantly interrupts the teacher. "The school principal wants a note from the doctor and will not allow Shawn back in the classroom until he is on a medication to calm him down."

"Do not touch anything!" She constantly admonishes the boy, who continues on doing what he was doing.

MELISSA

Melissa, a ten-year-old white girl, is brought by her mother to the behavioral pediatrics clinic because she is failing in school.

"Melissa is hyper, she acts silly to get everyone's attention, at times even by deliberately offending them, and, if nothing else works, by touching and pulling them," her mother says. "She constantly talks, interrupting others, and cannot wait for her turn."

She explains that, although Melissa is quick to respond, her answers are often thoughtless and wrong. "She forgets to bring her homework, and, if she does bring it, she either takes three or four hours to complete it or does not finish it at all. Her room is always like a pigpen. I have to ask her at least ten times before she does anything," her mother says. "No one likes her. She tries to boss other children around. When children do not let her play with them, she throws a tantrum."

Melissa rushes to give a warm hug to the doctor as soon as she enters the room. He disentangles himself gently, feeling uncomfortable at this exuberant display of affection by a child who does not know him. He requests her to draw a picture of her house and the people in it while he talks to her mother. Melissa then turns to the nurse, asking her name, why she is not wearing a white nurse's uniform, and what that thing is hanging on the wall. The nurse reminds her to draw what the doctor told her to draw. She innocently rests her head on her closed fist and says, "I forgot." Before the nurse can reply, Melissa interrupts the doctor, "What did you ask me to draw?" "Where are the crayons?" she asks the nurse without looking at the desk where the nurse had already put the crayons. While drawing, she constantly interrupts the doctor, saying "excuse me" every time. "Can I draw my dog also?" She leaves the drawing in the middle twice: once to check the door at which someone had knocked, and once to pick up the phone that rang. She crumples three papers before she completes her drawing. The picture she draws is chaotic, with too many people, things, and animals, each drawn hurriedly, with unnecessary shading. She asks the doctor, "Did I do good?" "Look mommy," she exclaims, "I drew my cat also. Can we go now?"

"Will you shut up!" her mother screams.

"How was she as a baby?" the doctor asks.

"Gee. She was a handful. She was a colicky baby. She kept me awake at nights. She was a terrible toddler, always running around, always saying 'No!'" the mother replies.

JASON

Jason, a twelve-year-old Hispanic child, is brought to the clinic because he is doing poorly in school and might be held back in the same class. The school wants to evaluate him for special education. His mother says that he is intelligent, but he does not put his mind to his work.

"He is a nice kid," the mother says. "The teacher is too old and doesn't know how to handle children. She wants to put everyone in special education. He is not hyper, he does not bother nobody, he is just lazy," his mother goes on.

The teacher, on the other hand, reports that Jason is inattentive and daydreams in the classroom. He often looks out the window instead of the blackboard, and he has to be reminded repeatedly to pay attention. He forgets to take notes from the blackboard and does not follow instructions. He fidgets and squirms in his seat, his desk is messy, and his pens and pencils keep falling off. So no one wants to sit next to him in the classroom.

Jason sits like an angel in the doctor's office, trying to draw a picture of a house, tree, and people in the house—but takes forever. He sometimes looks out the window, sometimes twiddles the crayons in his hands, and sometimes squirms in his chair. When the doctor asks him to show what he has drawn, he is startled as if he has been awakened from sleep. His drawing is incomplete.

❧

Are Shawn, Melissa, and Jason normal or abnormal? Healthy or sick?

It is difficult to draw a clear-cut line between normal and abnormal child behavior. All children are different and behave along a spectrum that ranges from normal to abnormal. Some children are noisy while some are calm, some are brash while some are polite, some are dynamic while some are passive, and some are gregarious while some are shy. Shawn could be a smart and curious child who wants to touch and feel everything in his environment. Melissa could be a socially immature girl who will mature with time, and Jason could be inattentive in the classroom because he is thinking about his future after his parents' impending divorce.

But the behaviors of Shawn, Melissa, and Jason are excessive, pervasive, and persistent. Shawn is so hyperactive that he cannot even eat his meals in peace; two adults cannot carry on a conversation when Melissa is around; and Jason has to be told at least ten times before he does anything. They display these behaviors everywhere: at home, in school, in restaurants, in the grocery store, and at their relatives' homes. They are failing in school and having problems with their teachers and peers. Their symptoms are not in response to a temporary stressor; they have always been like that. Shawn was kicked out of a day care program when he was three, and Melissa was a fussy infant who woke her neighbors on many nights. Their parents are stressed and are asking for help. These children have crossed the threshold of normalcy.

Could Shawn, Melissa, and Jason be acting willfully? Children, innately, want to please others; they yearn for approval and accolades. A two-month-old child looks intently at his mother's face, expecting a smile. He invites a response by smiling spontaneously, and if his mother returns the smile, he beams, vocalizes, and gurgles. A one-year-old looks at his mother for a "yea!" when he pops the jack-in-the-box the first time. A three-year-old looks around for claps when he completes a puzzle. A five-year-old wants a hug or a kiss from his mother when he recites a nursery rhyme. An eight-year-old wants a sticker from his teacher when he does his schoolwork well. Children are programmed to please others. They do not act bad intentionally, unless they are "driven" to do so by an underlying disease or condition. Shawn, Melissa, and Jason are not acting willfully; but they are behaving abnormally because they have an underlying behavioral disorder.

Diagnosis of behavioral disorders does not depend upon telltale signs that can be seen, touched, or heard with the stethoscope. It is inferential—an educated guess at best—based upon a constellation of observed behaviors. Isolated behaviors are not diagnostic, but when a set of behaviors occurs together at a degree and frequency such that the patient cannot do what is expected of him or her (for example, learn in school) or is not able to relate properly to people around him or her (parents, teachers, or peers), a behavior disorder is diagnosed.

The constellation of symptoms characteristic of various mental and behavioral disorders are published periodically by a national panel of psychiatrists in the United States in the *Diagnostic and Statistical Manual of Mental Disorders* or *DSM*. Although these diagnostic criteria are decided empirically, the validity of psychiatric disorders is confirmed by psychological and statistical techniques called *factor, cluster,* and *latent variable analysis.*

The children described above are not able to focus and maintain attention, and are easily distracted. All three are impulsive and two are hyperactive. While individually their symptoms are not diagnostic of any disease, together they constitute a disorder called *attention deficit disorder (ADD)* or *attention deficit hyperactive disorder (ADHD)*. ADD has been validated as a psychiatric disorder by the scientific techniques mentioned. Its major symptoms are described below:

1. **Attention deficit:** Attention deficit—or failure to attend to the task at hand—is the cardinal feature of this condition. The process of paying attention to a task involves getting tuned to a task and remaining focused until the goal is achieved. It is analogous to driving a car. It involves turning the ignition on (getting focused), putting the car (body and mind) in proper gear (proper level of arousal for the task), holding the steering wheel in constant check (staying focused), looking at the road ahead (vigilance), driving at the right speed (tempo), and reaching the goal without getting lost in the side lanes due to distractions (off-task activities). Another analogy is turning on the television (motivation and arousal), tuning to a channel (selectively attending), and staying on the channel until the show finishes (staying focused without being distracted). How much attention a child pays to a task depends upon the nature of the task. If a task is pleasing to the child, he or she will pay attention to it effortlessly. Most children are able to focus on a video game or a television show, because it gives them instant pleasure, inviting more viewing (a process called reinforcement). Moreover, these programs flood their senses with so much input—flooding the gates as it were—that other distractions cannot enter their brains. The litmus test of ADD is the inability to focus on homework or on a task that does not reward the children immediately. In the words of Russell Barkley,

author of *ADHD and the Nature of Self Control*, attention in ADD is more *context dependent* than internally guided.

Although not described in standard books on ADD, I have seen two types of inattentive children: children who cannot become focused on any task and those who cannot stay focused. I call the former the "failure-of-ignition" type, and the latter the "failure-to-drive" type. Failure-of-ignition-type children either wander aimlessly without doing anything meaningful or sit passively, looking out the window or twiddling their thumbs. They require constant reminders to begin a task, but may finish a task once they start. Failure-to-drive-type children leap like frogs from task to task, failing to finish anything they start. For example, a child comes to the doctor's office and excitedly begins to make a building with the Legos in the waiting room. He leaves the Legos after stacking a few blocks, makes a few strokes on a paper with a crayon, and then asks the secretary for a ball to play with. He bounces the ball three times, then asks the nurse for a book to read, turns a few pages of the book, and goes back to the drawing. Despite constant reminders, nothing is accomplished. Children who fail to sustain attention are easily bored and need a constant pep talk to keep up their rapidly fading interest. They burn out quickly. The speed and quality of their performance are very inconsistent, sometimes fast, sometimes slow, sometimes good, and sometimes poor. They lack the motivation to accomplish something in the distant future.

Children with ADD have difficulty in deciding which aspect of the environment is relevant to the goal at hand. This ability to select the salient activities pertaining to the goal at hand and to attend to them—the ability to sift chaff from grain—is called *selective attention*. Attention in a child matures from the exploratory, rapid, impulsive, divergent (interested in too many things at the same time), and reinforcement-based (requiring constant approval from the parents) to slow, deliberative, goal-directed, logical, and productive. A two-year-old child explores a toy, wants to push a pushcart, wants to grab a book that someone else is looking at—all at the same time. He constantly looks towards his parents for approval and praise (expects reinforcement and joint attention by his parents) after every little thing he does. Parents have to repeatedly say "Yea!" and clap if they want him to go on. A twelve-year-old child, on the other hand, sits at his desk, and slowly and logically finishes his homework without expecting constant approval from his parents at each step of the way.

The attentional skills of children with ADD do not mature according to this schedule. Their attention remains divergent and, instead of being driven internally by a goal, is driven by constant reinforcement from the environment (context- and contingency-based). Recently, a famous ADD researcher, Russell Barkley, has proposed that inattention is not the primary symptom of this condition, but a secondary effect of the child's failure to keep external factors in his or her environment from interfering with his or her attempts to sustain attention to achieve his or her goals.

2. Distractibility: Children with ADD have a tendency to get easily distracted by every little noise or movement in the surroundings. To sustain attention to a task, one has to literally shut the gates of the brain so that irrelevant stimuli received by the eyes and ears do not gatecrash into conscious awareness. Children with ADD are distracted by every sensation that reaches their five senses. Their situation is analogous to a radio that has "constant static" even when it is tuned to a particular station. A truck drives by on the road, and children with ADD run to the window, leaving their homework. Someone knocks at the door, and they are the first to ask "Who is there?" When there are no external distractions, they can have a state of internal distractibility; their *hyper minds* wandering all over the globe and daydreaming about known and unknown people, when they should be doing homework. No wonder people pejoratively call them scatterbrained, spaced-out, spacey, absent-minded, addlebrained, unfocused, and zoned-out.

The underlying neurological basis of distractibility in children with ADD seems to be a lack of sensory filtration at the level of the caudate nucleus (a group of nerve cells in the brain that acts as a relay station for all sensory input before it reaches conscious awareness). Normally, the *caudate nucleus* serves as a gatekeeper, allowing only relevant stimuli to reach conscious awareness. In children with ADD, the head of the right caudate nucleus is small, compared with normal children, and fails to inhibit the onslaught of input from various sense organs on the brain. Every stimulus makes it to conscious awareness.

3. Impulsivity: Children with ADD have a short circuit in their nerve-cell wiring, causing them to act impulsively, without thinking. They literally respond from the gut and not from the mind—and often wrongly. A child with ADD is often the first to raise his hand to answer the question, "Who is the president of the United States?" He may actually blurt out the answer without even raising his hand. An adolescent with ADD may mess up an appliance because he may turn it on without reading the instructions. Adults with ADD may buy stocks impulsively without knowing the fundamentals of the companies they are investing in because they heard someone in the elevator talking about a good buy. Individuals with ADD often get into trouble with the law because they act without thinking about the consequences of their actions. According to the famous ADD researcher Russell Barkley, this tendency in children with ADD to act impulsively rather than reflectively is due to poor working memory, resulting in poor processing of incoming information. Their working memory or, in computer language, random-access memory (RAM) cannot simultaneously hold information about prior experience with an action and its likely consequence. In other words, they have no forethought or afterthought.

A related deficit that results in impulsivity is the inability of children with ADD to delay gratification and wait for their turn. A child with ADD who goes to a restaurant with his parents cannot wait patiently to be served: He reminds the waiter many times despite his parents' admonition, twiddles with the silverware which finally falls to the ground, and finally gets up and pulls at the waitress's dress and demands that his food be served. A child with ADD who is brought to the doctor's office and is asked by the nurse to wait in the waiting hall asks her mother every five minutes when the doctor will see her, and finally knocks at the doctor's door to ask when it will be her turn. A child with ADD, promised a sticker by the doctor for reading quietly for fifteen minutes, will ask the doctor every minute, "Is it fifteen minutes yet?"

Researchers have shown that impulsivity is not a flaw of character but a defect of biology. Spontaneously hypertensive rats—whose behavior is similar to that of hyperactive children—performed better in an experimental task when they were rewarded immediately as compared with their nonhyperactive counterparts, the Wistar-Kyoto rats, who responded better when their reward was delayed. In an experiment, rats received water as a reward when they pressed a bar. Hyperactive rats responded faster when they received water immediately after pressing a bar, while the nonhyperactive rats responded faster when they received water after a longer interval. Methylphenidate administration reversed the situation, strengthening the response to delayed gratification.

4. Hyperactivity: Although generally considered to be the most salient feature of this disorder because of its obtrusiveness, this symptom is not present in all cases. Hyperactivity manifests in various ways: a) a macro form in which children are agitated, restless, and move constantly from place to place, touching people and things; b) a micro form in which children squirm and fidget in their seats; and c) a *hyperactive tongue* (or *hyper-tongue)* type in which children are garrulous, talking excessively, often out of context and interrupting others.

Macro-hyperactive children appear "driven by a motor." They cannot stay still. They walk over obstacles, unmindful of dangers. They run instead of walk. Micro-hyperactive children fidget and squirm like worms. No one likes to sit with them in the classroom. An adult with micro-hyperactivity will incessantly shake his legs while waiting in a doctor's office, and continually turn in his seat while watching a movie in the theater.

The hyper-tongue variety talk and talk, until someone shuts them up. They do not let anyone else talk in a conversation. A hyper-tongue raises her hand every time the teacher asks a question and opens her mouth before the teacher gives her permission to speak. She constantly interrupts her mom when her mother is talking to her friend, without saying "excuse me". When the mother admonishes her and tells her to say "excuse me," she continues to interrupt saying "excuse me." The exasperated mother has to say, "For God's sake, will you shut up?"

5. Deficits in the executive functions of the brain: Executive functions of the brain involve organization, self-monitoring, self-regulation, and continuous quality improvement—functions that a manager performs in an office. As children grow and develop, they learn to perform these functions. Children with ADD do not.

a) **Disorganization:** Children with ADD are not able to organize their space and time well. Their desks and rooms are disorganized. Jennie takes one hour to get going after she wakes up. Her room is a pigpen. Clothes are lying all over the floor and her books are all over her desk. She cannot find her books before she leaves for school and often forgets her books and dittos in school.

b) **Failure to self-monitor and self-regulate:** When Johnny walks, it seems as if the whole house is shaking, the roof rumbles, and the floor squeaks. When you tell him to walk gently because there are guests in the living room, he says "Sorry," ostensibly takes a few cautious steps, but soon goes back to his usual thunder. He comes barging into the living room complaining about his younger brother Tommy, who has taken his crayons from his room. His mother yells at him, "Don't you know that I have company?" He appears a little surprised, says he's sorry, but continues to complain loudly. He doesn't realize that he is screaming. The *servomechanism* that should give him feedback is not good enough. Lisa talks loudly. When she speaks, it seems as if she is yelling. But when you tell her to talk softly, she asks just as loudly, "Is that better now." The poor thing doesn't realize her volume is still up.

c) **Failure of continuous quality improvement:** Children with ADD are unable to learn from experience. Not only are they unable to monitor themselves, they do not respond to admonitions and advice from their parents. It is difficult for them to follow rules. In other words, they are hard to discipline, or "thickheaded." Parents often complain that the child does not listen; they feel that the child is deliberately trying to hurt their feelings and is disobedient. This results in conflicts with those in authority: parents and teachers. Once children organize their self-image around these negative behaviors, they deteriorate into oppositional, non-compliant and defiant children.

d) **Poor motor monitoring:** Many children with ADD are clumsy and accident-prone. They neither plan their movements properly nor execute them smoothly. As in many other spheres of their life, they cannot monitor their movements and the environment in which they move, tripping over bumps and falling into holes. Hyperactive children with autism and mental retardation are unaware of dangers.

e) Poor information management: Children with ADD process incoming information very superficially; things sink into their heads with difficulty. They often misinterpret what others say, resulting in conflicts. I once asked a child in my office to draw a picture of a house, tree and person. He said, "OK," and started drawing a picture of a character from the notorious television show *The Power Rangers.* When I reminded him that I wanted him to draw the picture of his house and the people in his house, he said, "Ooh, I forgot." They are not able to process the visual information that they get from others' body language, whether others are welcoming their interruption or are getting annoyed. Not only do they not process external information well, but they are unable to interpret the feedback their brain receives from their own ears, eyes, and body. For example, a child who is screaming at the top of his lungs may not be able to appreciate his mom's reprimand for screaming.

6. Deficits of social behavior: Most children with ADD have problems with understanding the social context and mood (poor social cognition) and are unable to match their behavior to it (poor social adaptability). In other words, they are socially inept: They do not understand whether the social mood is grim or jovial, they say and do what they have to say and do without understanding the social situation, they lack social grace, they are awkward and tactless, and they are intrusive and inopportune. These behaviors cause conflicts with their siblings and peers, make them unpopular, and can lead to their social rejection.

Kimmy Gibbler, a character in a popular prime-time television sitcom, *Full House,* is a typical intrusive child. She barges in any time she feels like, talking loudly, unmindful of what others are doing or saying. The famous television nerd of the sitcom *Family Matters,* Steve Urkel, is a perfect example of a child who lacks social intuition and social intelligence.

Other deficits in social behavior are given below:

a) Inability to follow instructions and rules: Children with ADD have difficulty following instructions. They do not understand rules, because i) they are so inattentive that they do not receive information properly, ii) they have difficulty processing the information they receive as instruction, or iii) their impulses make it difficult for them to follow the instructions. Parents often perceive this as opposition and defiance.

Rules are a set of instructions that a child is supposed to follow at home and in school. For example, a particular house may have a rule that children will put their toys in the toy chest before going to bed. Ordinarily, this instruction would become part of a child's behavioral dictionary after a few repetitions. In computer lingo, the program would be stored in their C: drive for ready retrieval whenever a situation clicks it to open. Children with ADD, however, will not be able to internalize it or store it in their C: drive. They may have to be told what is expected of them again and again. This may be a nuisance and an aggravation for parents.

b) Lack of hindsight and lack of foresight: Children with ADD have smaller working memory or, in computer language, smaller random-access memory (RAM) than other children. They can neither retrieve their past experience when faced with a situation, nor think about future consequences. This accounts for their failure to learn from past mistakes or to plan for the future. According to Russell Barkley, children with ADD live in the immediate present, from moment to moment, driven by their impulses and immediate responses to external stimuli.

c) Aggression: Children with uncomplicated ADD can indulge in random acts of aggression because of impulsivity and inability to think of the consequences of their actions. If a child indulges in aggressive acts in a deliberate and premeditated manner, the child is likely to have *conduct disorder* and should be seen by a psychiatrist.

d) Social immaturity: Children with ADD are often childish, comical, and clownish. They blame others for mistakes, are sensitive to criticism, do not accept responsibility for their actions, pout and sulk, and seek attention maladaptively, as a toddler would.

  i) Class clown: Johnny laughs, makes faces, grunts, and makes silly comments to seek attention. If no one pays attention, he does it more loudly and more obtrusively. When someone asks, "Are you a boy scout?", he says, "No, I am a poached egg" and then laughs. If you ignore him, he becomes increasingly disruptive, blows on your face, touches you, and so on, until you pay attention.

ii) "It's not me, it's them"—the blamer and pouter: Children with ADD tend to blame others for their behavior. For example, a child with ADD would blame his peers for his acts of aggression: "I hit him because he was bothering me"; "I yelled at the teacher because he was being mean to me." This phenomenon of blaming external things for our own actions is called *external locus of control.* Not only are their actions driven by external contexts and contingencies, their sense of responsibility is projected to others as well. They rarely accept moral responsibility for their actions.

2

Why Is It Difficult to Accept ADD as a Disease?

Children with ADD, like chameleons, change colors, behaving differently with different people (person-specific symptoms) in different situations (task-specific symptoms). For example, Johnny's parents bring him to see the doctor because he swirls like a top and moves like a whirlwind at home, but Johnny sits like an angel in the physician's office. The doctor concludes that nothing is wrong with Johnny. Charlie's mom is at her wit's end, because he does not listen to her and moves endlessly from one task to another without finishing anything while his dad is at work. When his dad comes home, Charlie stays still. Dad thinks that his wife does not know how to handle Charlie. The classroom teacher is pulling her hair out, because Jose talks endlessly in the class and keeps interrupting her, but he peacefully plays Nintendo or watches television at home. His parents think that his teacher is crazy.

The changing behavior of a child with ADD is not deliberate as it seems. The child's mind is conditioned to act freely with certain persons whom it considers benign and harmless. Failure to understand this can cause conflict between the mother and the father and between the parents and the teachers. Children with ADD may stay transfixed before their favorite television station for hours, but all hell breaks loose when they have to do homework. They itch, they have to go to the bathroom, they are hungry, they are distracted by every sound and sight in and around the house. They just cannot stay focused and still. As a rule, symptoms of ADD are increased in boring and nonstimulating situations, such as doing homework, and are decreased in stimulating and reinforcing situations, such as watching television or playing Nintendo. This variability confounds both parents and teachers into believing that the child is not doing homework deliberately, because he can pay attention when he wants to. This "doing versus driven" dilemma causes misunderstanding and conflict.

Performance slide and roller coaster performance over a period of time are hallmarks of ADD. Johnny starts off school enthusiastically getting A's, but, by the second marking period, he loses interest and is getting C's. Alternatively, he is getting A's one day and B's and D's the next day. ADD, true to its name, is a disorder, with no rules, consistency, or pattern. This performance attrition and inconsistency is a diagnostic criterion of ADD in the computerized continuous performance tests that are sometimes used to diagnose ADD.

The diagnosis of ADD is often delayed because of its changing symptoms. Parents keep vacillating between "our child is fine" and "our child has a disorder." Critics of ADD use this variability to prove that ADD is not a disease at all. They argue that if ADD were a disease, it would manifest under all situations, whether in school or at a party, with the father or with the mother, doing homework or playing a video game. However, ADD is not unique among diseases to have variable and intermittent symptoms. Despite an underlying tendency for asthma, asthmatic children wheeze only under certain circumstances, and symptoms can vary in severity from one episode to another. We do not, however, brush aside asthma as a disease, nor do we blame parents of asthmatics for poor parenting because they allowed their children to be exposed to allergens, dust, and fumes. Migraine is intermittent, and so is epilepsy. Symptoms of other behavior disorders, such as depression and schizophrenia, wax and wane, too.

Symptoms of ADD are believed to change in different seasons as well, arising more in spring and winter. I see a surge in requests for appointments and prescriptions for medications in the spring, the final marking period in schools and when demands on children and parents are high. In summer, children can go outdoors away from their parents and sweat it all out, while in winter they remain huddled in the house, close to their parents, making the parents more aware of their children's shortcomings.

The whimsically-changing behavior of children with ADD is very stressful for their parents, siblings, and teachers. It is difficult to relate to a child who behaves like an angel one moment, and like a devil the next. I remember a mother who consulted me about her daughter's inattentive and hyperactive behavior. She was ambivalent about her daughter's behavior: it was very inconsistent—good on some days and bad on others. "I think she is behaving like this because I have been very busy for the past month or so, and her dad, too, has been preoccupied with his business. I do not understand. Some days she is so nice. She listens to me and helps me with chores. Other days she is wild, irritable, and moody. Wouldn't she be 'bad' all the time if she had ADD? No, I am not going to give her medicine."

I suggested a few techniques of behavior modification to her, gave her the parent and the teacher versions of the Conners questionnaire, and rescheduled her. Conners questionnaire, developed by a famous ADD researcher, Dr. Keith Conners, is one of many questionnaires that are used to obtain information about a child's behavior in a structured manner. This mother called me the next week to tell me that her daughter was behaving very well, almost like a different person, since she had seen me. It was like a happy ending—too good to be true. Two weeks later, I was paged by my secretary for an emergency. She informed me that the child's mother urgently wanted an appointment to see me. Her daughter had been suspended from school. The child had been very hyperactive, disrupting the class, and had pushed another child down the stairs during recess.

3

Is ADD a New Disorder?
THE JOURNEY OF ADD THROUGH TIME

Attention deficit disorder (ADD)—also known as attention deficit hyperactivity disorder (ADHD)—is not a new disorder. (As I mentioned in the Preface, I will refer to both as ADD rather than swim around in acronyms.) In 1845, Heinrich Hoffmann, a physician in Frankfurt, published a book of stories about children who, like children with ADD, were hyperactive, fidgety, and clumsy. Of the character "Fidgety Philip", he writes: "Let me see if he is able to sit still for once at the table, he wriggles, and giggles, swings backwards and forwards and tilts up his chair." Of "Unkempt Peter", or *Struwwelpeter*, he writes: "There he stands, with his nasty hair and hands. See! His nails are never cut."

Pearl, the impish elf of Nathaniel Hawthorne's *Scarlet Letter* reminds one of a child with ADD: "She now skipped irreverently from one grave to another. There is no law, nor reverence for authority ... mixed up with that child's composition. The child could not be made amenable to any rules, a being whose elements were perhaps beautiful and brilliant, but all in disorder. A child whose activity of spirit never flagged, a child of fitfully capricious temper."

Although this disorder has been with us, perhaps since the beginning of civilization, various explanations have been offered for it from time to time. In biblical times, one with bad behavior was considered to be smitten by Satan. At the turn of this past century (1902), Dr. George Frederick Still, a famous British pediatrician credited with describing arthritis in children, reported children with behaviors similar to ADD and attributed their behavior to "morbid defects in moral control." In the first half of the twentieth century, there was major shift in thinking about behavioral problems, from moral to psychological, due to the pioneering work of Sigmund Freud. According to Dr. Freud, most abnormal behaviors were due to repressed conflicts and previous psychic trauma.

This tendency to attribute abnormal behaviors to past emotional trauma continued until the 1950s when two researchers, Laufer and Denhoff, suggested that the abnormal behaviors that characterized ADD were due to neurological dysfunction. They arrived at this conclusion because many children suffering from this *symptom complex* had subtle neurological signs, such as, clumsiness and inability to balance on one foot or to walk in a straight line. Other neurologists hypothesized that this neurological dysfunction resulted from minimal brain damage sustained by the child during the process of birth (reproductive casualty). This theory of minimal brain damage was supported by the high prevalence of this symptom complex in survivors of encephalitis lethargica, a viral infection of the brain. Although the concept of minimal brain damage was not specific to ADD, it marked a watershed shift from psychodynamically based explanations—"doing bad"—for abnormal behavior to neurologically based explanations—"driven to do bad". Because no evidence of brain damage was seen on CT scans of the brain, the name of the condition was changed from "minimal brain damage" to "minimal brain dysfunction."

However, because of the behavioral nature of symptoms, ADD returned to the domain of psychiatry in the 1970s when the American Psychiatric Association appointed a panel of experts to lay down criteria for the diagnosis of behavioral conditions. These criteria, published by the American Psychiatric Association in the *Diagnostic and Statistical Manual of Mental Disorders* (*DSM-III, DSM-III-R,* and *DSM-IV*), included ADD as a psychiatric disorder and stressed that attention deficit 'or inability to focus', and not hyperactivity, is the cardinal symptom of this disorder. Children may not be hyperactive and yet may have this disorder if they are inattentive. Therefore, this disorder was renamed attention deficit disorder and, later, attention deficit hyperactivity disorder.

Nowadays, this disorder is being redefined as a disorder of the executive functions of the brain—such as planning of actions and tailoring them to the ultimate goals—and a disorder of behavioral inhibition—an inability to avoid responding to rewarding but counterproductive stimuli (according to Russell Barkley). The journey of ADD through time is far from over.

4

How Common Is ADD Anyway?

According to most studies in the United States, ADD occurs in one of twenty school-age children. However, recent studies from Puerto Rico and Canada report an even higher prevalence of one in every ten children. According to the US Department of Education, nearly 2.5 million children under the age of 18 in the United States have ADD.

Skeptics argue that one-tenth of the country's children cannot be afflicted with a behavioral disorder. According to these critics, either this disorder is not valid or too many children are being wrongly diagnosed as suffering from it. However, the common occurrence of a disease does not make it invalid. Millions of people suffer from arthritis, but that does not make it a fake disorder. If self-control were a natural instinct or trait, as some researchers believe, it would be distributed according to the famous bell-shaped curve, and about 2.5 percent of individuals would have significantly low levels of self-control. Even detractors of ADD, such as Professor Carey of the Children's Hospital of Philadelphia, accept that one-to-two percent of children may be so unmanageable that they qualify for the diagnosis of ADD. Although the anti-ADD lobby is using these spiraling numbers to refute ADD, two renowned psychiatrists—Dr. Joseph Biederman of the Harvard Medical School and Dr. Larry Silver, author of *Attention Deficit Disorder: A Clinical Guide to Diagnosis and Treatment* (American Psychiatric Press, 1992)—feel that ADD is still underdiagnosed.

Is the prevalence of ADD truly rising, or is ADD being diagnosed more often? There has been a doubling of the number of children with the diagnosis of ADD every four to seven years in Baltimore County, where, in 1987, about six percent of all public elementary school children were receiving stimulant medication. According to the National Ambulatory Care Survey for the years 1990 to 1995, the number of office visits with the diagnosis of ADD has increased from 947,208 in 1990 to 2,357,833 in 1995: a 2.3-fold increase. According to Ronald Hoffman, MD, the author of *The Natural Approach to Attention Deficit Disorder (ADD): Drug-Free Ways to Treat the Roots of This Childhood Epidemic*, ADD is being diagnosed more often now because of increased public awareness of this disorder.

The information explosion in the latter half of this century has made ADD a household word. In the United States, ADD has become a political battleground with the religious right and disciplinarians on the one side and scientists and psychiatrists on the other. Political battles are media staples, and this media hype has made ADD a popular disease. It has become the butt of many a joke and has found itself a place in comic strips. Every parent and every teacher is aware of it. Whereas pediatricians in the past rarely diagnosed this disorder, today every pediatrician has a few children with ADD in his or her panel of patients.

Higher societal expectations of children—in and out of the classroom—are also contributing to ADD being diagnosed more often than it used to be. Whereas, in the past, hyperactive and inattentive children were able to leave the school and "find their niche" in some trade or other, now every child has to cope with school through high school. Natalie Angier wrote in the *New York Times* in 1994, "...a generation or two ago, a guy with a learning disability—or an ornery temperament—could drop out of school, pick up a trade and become, say, the best bridge builder in town. Now, if a guy can't manage to finish college [he is out of luck]." Even today in some countries, children with ADD have a way out of the classroom to a workshop a farm, or a factory. Similarly, in the past, active children could move out of their house into the extended family network. Now they stay cooped up in their nuclear families with no respite for their parents. Tom Sawyer and Huckleberry Finn, the darlings of America, today would not be able to leave their homes and have an adventure; instead, they would be identified as having a psychiatric disorder and taken for testing and counseling.

Although greater awareness of ADD and a rush to diagnose it are self-evident, it is difficult to prove that there has been a true increase in the prevalence of ADD. It is unlikely that the biological factors that underlie ADD have increased. There are many social and environmental factors in the United States and other developed countries that could trigger the underlying biological vulnerabilities and create a poor fit between children and their environment, creating a state of "dis-ease" or "dis-order."

Today, a child in the western world—especially in the United States—is bombarded by television and other media from daybreak until bedtime. Many of the programs for children—especially the cartoons—are very noisy, with quick changes of scene. Sitcoms show characters who run instead of walk, shout and argue instead of talk, and express their emotions histrionically, accompanied by laugh tracks. However, scientific studies do not show a consistent effect of television viewing and television quality on children's attention and task perseverance. In an experiment in which children were assigned to watch one hour of fast-paced programming and one hour of slow-paced programming, there were no effects on subsequent attention or perseverance. In 1988, two researchers, Anderson and Collins, reviewed the extant literature on television and thinking and problem-solving abilities (*cognitive processing*) for the US Department of Education and concluded that there was little evidence to support the idea that television as a medium had any effect on cognitive processes, such as attention, impulsivity, or attention span.

The pace of life, too, is very fast in the United States, with both parents rushing, huffing, and puffing all the time. Being loud and vocal is considered more valuable today than being soft-spoken and taciturn. Maybe children whose innate ability to modulate responses to environmental inputs is limited cannot cope with the overstimulation. With the easy availability of high-speed computers and electronic remote controls, children do not have to wait for anything. Therefore, when they have to wait for their turn, it is an anathema to them, a sign of organizational dysfunction. In her review of the book *Faster: The Acceleration of Just About Everything* by James Gleick, *New York Times* columnist Barbara Ehrenreich asks what is happening to our attention spans in this "multiple-interfacing, hyper-wired" world. According to her, we lose "the chance to reflect, to analyze, when just about everything" accelerates. "Unfortunately, deep concentrated thought is not as fast as an electron tunneling through silicon. Like composting, it takes time. Try to shorten that time and you move very quickly from diverting to distracted," she says.

Lack of parental control and too much autonomy for children are also cited as being responsible for the higher prevalence of behavior problems in children in the United States. Although there is no evidence that a laissez faire attitude towards parenting can cause ADD, it can certainly increase the expression of disease. Whereas in other countries children may be inhibited because of parental authority and the ability to give physical punishment, in the United States children have a long rope before their parents will do or say anything to them. Children show their true colors under these conditions.

Whatever may be the cause—an innate inability to regulate behavior, behavioral disequilibrium due to "ADD-ogenic" culture, or unregulated behavior due lack of parental control—ADD is a very common disorder in the United States. The fact that our culture is ADD-genic does not invalidate ADD as a disease, just as the high prevalence of heart disease in the United States does not invalidate it as a disease, even though our diet is heart-disease-ogenic. However, the phenomenon of ADD should be studied across different cultures and countries to identify those environmental and sociocultural conditions that are associated with a high prevalence of ADD. Once these factors are identified, we can work to decrease the prevalence of ADD by controlling these factors.

5

Is ADD a Disease of the Affluent?

ADD is not a disease of affluence. It is found in all social and economic classes. During my clinical practice in and around New York, I have seen ADD in East Harlem, in the South Bronx, in the North Bronx and in Westchester County, New York, as well as in Bergen County, New Jersey. I have seen ADD in children of women living in shelters, in children of welfare recipients who can barely make ends meet, and in children of physicians living in the exclusive high-rise apartment buildings on Park Avenue in New York City. One-fifth of the children in a study on ADD conducted by the US National Institute of Mental Health (NIMH) were receiving welfare or public assistance.

ADD occurs in children of all races and cultures: Caucasians, African-Americans, East Europeans, Latinos, Asians, Haitians, and Africans. In a study at multiple pediatric practices in the United States, ADD was found to occur in children of all races and classes. There was no difference in prevalence among blacks and whites, although slightly lower prevalence was noticed among Asians and Native Americans.

ADD is not due to cultural maladaptation to the pressures of American urban life. If this were true, ADD would occur only after a child and his family have lived in the United States for some time. But I have seen ADD in children of recent Mexican immigrants and in children of parents from the coast of West Africa who live for part of the year in the United States and the rest in Africa. No difference has been found in the prevalence of ADD in urban and rural areas of the United States.

ADD is not limited to the United States, but has been reported in the United Kingdom, Canada, Australia, Spain, and Germany—a further proof of its biological nature. The reported prevalence in Europe and Australia is, however, much lower than in the United States, because of more a conservative approach of physicians to diagnosis and treatment of ADD in those countries. However, similar rates emerge if questionnaire surveys of teachers are used to estimate prevalence. In a multinational study of the United States, United Kingdom, New Zealand, Australia, and Germany, Patricia Holborow and Paul Berry of the University of Queensland, Australia, found similar rates of abnormal scores in teacher-reported questionnaires. According to their findings, the variation in the prevalence of ADD across countries is, quoting an earlier study by R. Glow, "an artifact of diagnostic decision process."

Although many consider ADD to be a disease of western civilization, classroom pressures and a closer scrutiny of children's behavior is resulting in an escalation of the number of children identified with ADD in urban centers of developing countries, such as China, Hong Kong, India, and Brazil. In these countries, ADD has not reached the epidemic proportion that it has in the United States, perhaps because of lower acceptance of abnormal behaviors of children as symptoms of diseases and less availability of mental health services.

"Do parents have any important long-term effects on the development of their children's personality? ...the answer is no"

JUDITH RICH HARRIS, *The Nurture Assumption*

6

Does Bad Parenting Cause ADD?

ADD is not caused by inadequate or improper parenting. Unfortunately, few studies have addressed the question of the type of parents, type of parenting, and type of families associated with ADD. There is, however, no characteristic profile of a parent of a child with ADD, and all types of parenting styles are seen among parents of children with ADD: permissive, punitive, restrictive, authoritative, and authoritarian. Even if a particular behavioral profile of parents is found to be associated with ADD, it would be difficult to establish whether the parents' behavior caused ADD or ADD in the child prompted the parents to behave in that manner—the chicken-and-egg dilemma. Two identical twins reared in different homes, behave similarly, suggesting that heredity plays a bigger role in the causation of ADD than parenting. Two children raised by the same parents in an apparently similar manner often turn out to be different, once again suggesting that heredity has stronger role than parenting in the causation of ADD. Peer influence, too, does not appear to be a cause of ADD. Symptoms of ADD surface in toddler years, when children still spend most of their time with their parents and peers have not become an important aspect of their lives. It is likely that children with ADD, in school years, select and hang out with peers who meet their behavioral profile.

Theorists from both sides of the parenting aisle—the disciplinarians and the lenient—blame parents for disruptive behavior of their children. The disciplinarians argue that lenient parents spoil their children by not setting appropriate limits, and the lenient contend that punitive parents provide aggressive models for their children to emulate. The prophets of permissive parenting, Benjamin Spock and Selma Fraiberg, contend that children whose parents are not responsive to their needs in their formative years learn not to be responsive to the needs of others when they grow up. Selma Fraiberg, in *The Magic Years,* argues that "the ability to control impulse, to triumph over body urges" is dependent "on ties to the human educator." She states that "those mental qualities that we call 'human' are not part of the constitutional endowment of the infant, are not as instinctive as are the characteristic of other animals, and will not be acquired simply through maturation." Although her method of teaching "the quality of love that transcends love of self" is permissive, it sets the stage for blaming parents if their children turn out otherwise impulsive and intemperate. Both her premises—that the infants are not endowed with human qualities and that impulse control and self-regulation is a learned behavior—have not been confirmed, but they have greatly influenced the thinking of the baby-boomers that everything that goes wrong with their children is their parents' wrongdoing—the parents were not good enough.

Disciplinarians argue that much of the misbehavior that we see in children in the United States today is due to "too much freedom and autonomy." They cite the lower frequency of behavior problems among children in the Asian countries and in Asian-American children in the United States to support an authoritarian style of parenting. John Rosemond, their messiah, says that ADD is not genetic and "parents who pay attention to their children's proper brain development—by shielding them from electronic media, making them focus on adult authority figures and expecting them to finish tasks—cause this innate ADD to disappear." This assertion is too simplistic and is not supported by research. A group of psychologists at Vanderbilt University, Nashville, Tennessee, found that harsh disciplining by the mother in early years was associated with disruptive behavior later. Another group of psychologists reached a similar conclusion after studying 1,056 mothers of children who were one to five years of age from a large Midwestern urban population.

However, even this research is flawed because it does not resolve the chicken-and-egg dilemma. Children with difficult temperaments and behavior problems are likely to be disciplined more harshly than their easier counterparts. Researchers should take into account the overall culture and parent-child relations, as well. In cultures where physical disciplining is the norm, it is likely to have less impact upon children than where verbal explanations and behavioral contingencies are preferred. Harsh disciplining is likely to have more devastating effect in children whose parents are generally neglectful, as compared to those whose parents provide ample educational and recreational opportunities.

This "nurture assumption," in the words of Judith Harris, has gone too far. The parents of Eric Harris and Dylan Kleebold are being sued for what their children did at Columbine High. "This 'there must be someone to blame' mentality assumes a simple cause-and-effect relationship in parenting," writes a reader (Laura A. Watt) in a letter to editor published in the *New York Times Magazine*. "In reality, people are wildly complex creatures," she continues. And this seems to be the crux of the problem. The relation between parenting style and behavior problems in children is not as simple as the neo-disciplinarians or their nemesis—permissive parenting—experts would have you believe. Children are born with innate vulnerabilities and abilities inherited from their parents, but these vulnerabilities and abilities express themselves in a social milieu consisting of their parents, siblings, peers, cyber-peers, and teachers. Genes and environment interact with each other: a "strong-willed child" elicits harsher discipline, a resilient child withstands many foster care placements, a poorly endowed child selects other underachievers as his peers, a well-endowed child is damaged because he is exposed to substances in the womb or is born premature. The scenario is simply too complex to lend itself to simple solutions. To ascribe ADD to poor parenting in this scenario is like holding up one piece of a jigsaw puzzle and declaring that it is solved.

*"Is the mental disorder due to a chemical disorder?
And, is the chemical disorder due, in its turn, to psychological
distresses affecting the adrenals?"*

ALDOUS HUXLEY, *The Doors of Perception*

7

What Is Wrong with the ADD Brain?
The Neurological Basis of ADD

The neurological basis of ADD is still not fully known. Much of the
available evidence points to a deficiency or imbalance of one or more of the
neurotransmitters in the brain. Neurotransmitters are chemicals that, like errand
boys, carry the message of one brain cell (neuron) to another across the tiny
space between them called the *synaptic cleft* (Figure 1).

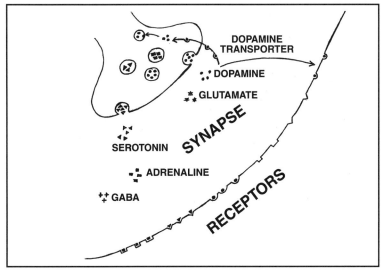

Figure 1

Brain cells store these neurotransmitters in tiny vesicles, ready to be discharged upon command. Once discharged, they attach themselves to specific areas, called *receptors*, on the surface of the brain cell across the cleft. The union of a neurotransmitter with its specific receptor triggers some changes in the receiving brain cell, either stimulating it or inhibiting it. Thus, the neurotransmitters serve as the currency of thoughts and emotions in the human brain. Once their job is done, neurotransmitters are transported back into the sending neuron where they are repackaged as vesicles, a process called *reuptake*.

The most popular, and perhaps the most plausible, theory of ADD is that it occurs due to a deficiency or dysfunction of the neurotransmitter dopamine in those areas of the brain that regulate attention and activity. The exact nature of the defect is unknown. The proposed theories include defects in the synthesis, storage, release, and reuptake of dopamine, and changes in the sensitivity of dopamine receptors. Researchers have found abnormalities in the concentration of metabolites (waste products) of dopamine in the blood and spinal fluid of a few children with ADD. For example, Dr. Xavier Castellanos, a researcher at the National Institute of Medicine, has found that the levels of homovanillic acid (HVA), a metabolite of dopamine, fail to decrease with age in children with ADD, as normally happens. Therefore, the child continues to behave as a younger child would. However, these findings are not consistent and constant. The drug

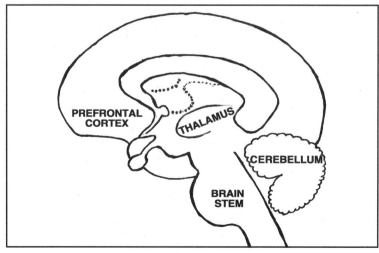

Figure 2

methylphenidate (Ritalin) is believed to enhance the release and uptake of dopamine.

Further evidence of the malfunction of dopamine neurons in ADD comes from animal models. Newborn rats become intensely hyperactive when their dopamine fibers are destroyed by 6-hydroxydopamine, a chemical that selectively damages dopaminergic fibers. This hyperactivity can be reduced by the administration of dextroamphetamine, a drug used to treat ADD.

Regions of the brain that are involved in regulating attention are the prefrontal cortex, the caudate nucleus, the thalamus, and the nucleus accumbens (see Figure 2). There is some evidence from studies in animals that dopaminergic activity in the prefrontal cortex enhances attention and decreases motor activity. Whereas attention improves directly as a result of dopaminergic activity in the prefrontal cortex, motor activity is decreased through an inhibitory influence on the release of dopamine in a deeper structure in the brain called nucleus accumbens (Figure 3). It is postulated that dopamine activity in the prefrontal cortex is decreased in children with ADD, resulting in inattention and hyperactivity. Using brain-imaging techniques—such as magnetic resonance imaging (MRI), positron emission tomography (PET) and single photon emission computed tomography (SPECT)—it has been shown that the right prefrontal cortex and the caudate nucleus are smaller in some individuals with ADD and that there is decreased chemical activity during tasks requiring attention in the prefrontal cortex of individuals with ADD, lending support to this theory.

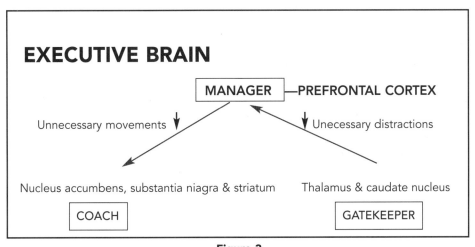

Figure 3

The prefrontal cortex is also connected to the thalamus, which serves as the relay station for all the sensory stimuli that arrive in the brain. The thalamus serves to filter the relevant or salient stimuli from noise or irrelevant stimuli and allows only the relevant stimuli to reach conscious awareness. The prefrontal cortex enhances this activity by releasing dopamine through neural pathways. In children with ADD, this "gatekeeper" role of the thalamus is impaired so that every stimulus—relevant or irrelevant—reaches conscious awareness, distracting the child from the work at hand.

Some researchers believe that two other neurotransmitters—noradrenaline and serotonin—are also involved in children with ADD. The levels of methoxy-hydroxyphenylglycol, a metabolite of noradrenaline, have been reported to be low in some children with ADD. According to some scientists, the symptoms of ADD vary depending on which neurotransmitter system is involved predominantly: deficits in dopamine, noradrenaline, and serotonin cause the inattentive, hyperactive, and impulsive types of ADD, respectively.

According to another group of researchers, ADD is due to an imbalance of chemicals in the two halves of the brain, characterized by reduced dopamine in the left half of the brain and increased noradrenaline in the right half of the brain. Because the left hemisphere is concerned with focusing attention on specific tasks, decreased function therein results in the inattentive type of ADD. The right hemisphere is concerned with attending to a wider space, so increased noradrenergic activity in the right brain increases general wakefulness and attention to unimportant stimuli in the environment, resulting in distractibility and hyperactivity. Hyperactivity occurs because the prefrontal cortex—sometimes called the managerial module of the brain—is lazy in inhibiting a hyperactive child's urge to move. Additionally, excessive noradrenergic activity puts the hunter-gatherer right brain on hyperalert, increasing distractibility.

A few detractors of ADD argue against this biological model (Peter Breggin, Lawrence Diller), as if the mind were some nebulous ethereal entity separate from the body. Mind is rooted in biology. Each thought, each feeling, and each behavior has a chemical change or an electrical reaction in the brain as its substrate. The future of psychiatry lies in discovering these substrates and treating them. And if the problem is chemical, so is likely to be its solution.

*"Emotional problems rarely have a simple cause;
the difficulties result from complex interactions among
biological, psychological, and social factors."*

STANLEY TURECKI, MD

8

What Causes ADD?

The diagnosis of ADD raises more questions than it answers. Parents ask, "What did we do wrong? Why us?" Conditioned to attribute a cause to every effect, they embark on a wild-goose chase to assign a cause. The husband accuses his wife: "My son has ADD because you were smoking during pregnancy." The wife retorts: "It is because you used to argue with me." The grandmother blames "all them candies that Johnny eats." The grandfather, an injury attorney, believes that it is due to mismanagement of labor and delivery. The aunt, a freelance journalist, blames media violence and the New Age culture for her nephew's ADD. Mr. Brown, the charlatan on the block, wants to rid the body of all the toxins produced by fungus overgrowth in the gut; and Ms. Garbo, the faith healer, wants to exorcise the body of the evil spirits that are occupying it. There are as many supposed causes as there are mouths.

This situation occurs in ADD because the exact cause of ADD is still unknown, and because emotions are stronger than the principles of logic that determine causation. Overgeneralization—such as, all chickens die when they cross Willow Road because one chicken died when he crossed Willow Road in 1910—is common. Pseudologic—such as, Willow Road is the cause of death, because a chicken died while crossing it—prevails. This pseudologic is promoted by hearsay, emotion-laden anecdotes, and colorful Web pages.

In this book, I make no claim to know the truth, because the truth is as yet unknown. I do, however, discuss those theories of causation of ADD for which some scientific support is available. None of the proposed causes discussed below invariably precede or occur with ADD, as should happen in a true cause-and-effect scenario. Hence the term "theory". Perhaps many roads lead to the final pathway of ADD. Alternatively, ADD is caused by a number of factors working together, in concert or tandem.

Minimal brain damage: This theory was proposed in the 1960s by a few neurologists who suggested that ADD, like other disabling conditions—such as cerebral palsy and mental retardation—is caused by brain damage sustained by the child during the process of birth. Brain damage responsible for ADD was considered to be minimal because no changes are seen on CT scan and MRI of the brain of individuals with ADD, and most cases do not have a history or physical findings suggestive of brain damage. Although this theory is fashionable in the legal community, it is not based on evidence. Most children with ADD have normal birth histories, and most children with abnormal birth histories do not have ADD. ADD is common in preterm children and in children exposed to alcohol and, according to some researchers, cocaine during pregnancy. There are a few studies that relate maternal cigarette smoking during pregnancy to ADD. However, not all children exposed to alcohol, cocaine, or nicotine during pregnancy are hyperactive and inattentive, and a good environment can mitigate the effects of these substances to some extent.

Major brain damage caused by conditions such as birth trauma, birth asphyxia, and traumatic head injury can be associated with ADD. Damage to the brain is visible on the CT scan or MRI of the brain in such cases, and causes mental retardation, epilepsy, and cerebral palsy as well.

Heredity: Heredity is the process of passing the characteristics of the parents to their children. The blueprint of our characteristics resides in genes that are located in the thread-like structures called chromosomes that reside in each of our cells. This passage of genes occurs through the egg of the mother and the sperm of the father. That heredity causes ADD is suggested by the following observations:

1. ADD is five times more common in parents, siblings, and other first-degree relatives of individuals with ADD than in the general population. Other behavioral disorders—such as conduct disorder (in which children are aggressive or disruptive, break societal rules, and impinge on others' rights), oppositional disorder (in which children do the opposite of what

the authority figure asks), and depression—are also common among first-degree relatives of patients with ADD. However, it is difficult to separate the effect of environment (nurture) from the effect of heredity (nature). Dysfunctional relatives in the family may set a bad example for a child to emulate. Alternatively, those with abnormal behavior share certain abnormal genes.

2. Adoption studies suggest that ADD is more common in biological relatives than in adoptive relatives, suggesting that biology is more important than environment in causing ADD.

3. Studies of twins report higher rates of *concordance* for ADD among monozygotic twins (one-egg twins) than fraternal twins (two-egg twins). Concordance means the presence of a disease in both members of a twin pair. If a disease were genetic, there would be higher concordance in identical twins, because they have identical genes. If, on the other hand, a disease were due to environmental factors, the rates of ADD would be similar in all twins, identical or fraternal, because they share the same environment. Higher rates of ADD among identical twins suggest that genes are more important than environment in the causation of ADD.

4. Children with certain genetic conditions are more prone to ADD. Examples include Fragile X syndrome, Williams syndrome, and an extremely rare disorder of generalized resistance to thyroid hormone. All these conditions have other signs and symptoms besides ADD, and, therefore, routine genetic testing of hyperactive children for these syndromes is not warranted. Similarly, testing for abnormalities of thyroid hormone should be done only if there are signs of thyroid disease.

Despite some evidence of the contribution of hereditary factors in the causation of ADD, a gene for ADD has not been discovered. Geneticists are looking for abnormalities in the genes that control the formation of dopamine transporter and D4 receptor. Abnormalities in either of these substances can decrease the levels of dopamine in the synaptic cleft between nerve cells. Until a definite gene can be identified for ADD, only children with facial or other abnormalities suggestive of genetic conditions such as Fragile X or Williams syndrome's should be seen by genetic disease specialists.

I want to end this discussion about the role of heredity in ADD on a note of caution. The contribution of heredity in ADD is so uncertain at present that parents should not rush to judgment and blame each other for their child's ADD.

Environment: Although ADD and learning disability (LD) are more prevalent among children of poor and poorly educated parents, there is little evidence that poverty causes ADD. The higher prevalence of ADD among low socioeconomic children is perhaps due to the phenomenon of social drifting. Individuals with ADD and LD tend to move lower on the social ladder because of lower income. They tend to bear children with ADD and LD because of the influence of heredity. A poor and disorganized environment, in turn, causes further deterioration of their condition, creating a vicious cycle. Chaos begets chaos. Children from poor, overcrowded, and disorganized homes learn to be disorganized, noisy, and loud (social learning). They cultivate the traits of distractibility and impulsivity, because these traits give them a defensive edge in the predatory environment of the ghetto. However, not all children of poverty grow up to be hyperactive and disorganized. Many are resilient and come out with flying colors, depending on the relative strength of nature over nurture.

The issue of psychosocial adversity and mental disorders has been examined by British psychiatrist Sir Michael Rutter. Rutter proposed that a combination of adverse familial and environmental factors (severe marital discord, low social class, large family size, paternal criminality, maternal mental disorder, and foster care placement), rather than any single factor, is associated with behavior problems in children. Harvard psychiatrist Joseph Biederman, in a study, found support for Rutter's hypothesis in that a combination of adverse familial factors was associated with increased risk for ADD, but noticed that psychosocial adversity increased not only the risk of ADD, but of non-ADD mental disorders as well.

Other associations: Stress during pregnancy has also been shown to be associated with ADD in the children, either directly by causing preterm birth, indirectly, or by creating a dysfunctional family environment that continues beyond pregnancy.

Anemia caused by lack of iron in the diet was proposed as a cause of inattention by a famous US hematologist, Dr. Frank Oski. Anemia may cause inattention due to listlessness and lack of energy, but does not cause other symptoms of ADD. Seizure medications—such as Phenobarbital—and asthma medications—such as albuterol and theophylline—can cause restlessness and agitation as side effects.

Very high levels of lead in the blood are sometimes associated with symptoms of ADD, but lower levels do not cause this problem. A few nutritionists have found lower levels of essential fatty acids in some children with ADD, but it is not clear if the deficiency causes the symptoms or is merely associated with ADD by chance.

"It may be true that in flipping through the DIAGNOSTIC AND STATISTICAL MANUAL OF MENTAL DISORDERS, *a casual reader could probably find a single symptom like ...hyperactivity that fits his behavior...on any given day. However, mental disorders are defined by a cluster of symptoms that are sufficiently severe to impair normal functioning or interfere with daily activities."*

MICHAEL B. FIRST, MD
Letter to Editor, The New York Times, December 17, 1999

9

How Is ADD Diagnosed?

ADD defies the one-disease/one-cause model; and the multitude of factors that contribute to ADD are not known so well that they can be identified by diagnostic tests. ADD is not caused by a bug whose presence can be detected by a throat culture or a blood test; it is not caused by a dysfunction of the lungs that can be detected by an x-ray; and it is not caused by a lesion of the brain that can be detected by a CT scan or MRI of the brain. The imbalance of neurotransmitters in the tiny clefts between nerve cells of the brain of individuals with ADD is not reflected in blood tests. Thus, there is no laboratory test that can diagnose ADD.

Diagnosis of ADD is made clinically—as an art—by obtaining reports of the child's behavior from his parents and teachers. ADD is diagnosed if a child has symptoms and signs of ADD as laid down in the *Diagnostic and Statistical Manual of Mental Disorders* (popularly called *DSM-IV*). *DSM-IV* lists the symptoms of various mental disorders agreed upon by an expert panel of psychiatrists belonging to the American Psychiatric Association.

The symptoms of ADD consist of two categories of nine symptoms each. The first category has nine symptoms of inattention and distractibility, and the second category has six symptoms of hyperactivity and three symptoms of impulsivity.

The symptoms of inattention include the following: failing to give close attention to details or making careless mistakes in schoolwork or other activities; difficulty in sustaining attention in tasks or play activities; failure to listen when spoken to directly; difficulty in following through on instructions from others; difficulty in organizing tasks and activities; avoiding tasks that require sustained mental effort (such as schoolwork or homework); losing things necessary for tasks or activities; forgetfulness and easy distractibility.

The symptoms of hyperactivity/impulsivity are the following: fidgeting with hands or squirming when seated; subjective feelings of restlessness; difficulty in taking turns in games and other group activities; shifting from one uncompleted activity to another; difficulty in playing quietly; engaging in physically dangerous activities without considering possible consequences; blurting out answers to questions before they have been completed; interrupting others; and talking excessively.

A child is diagnosed to have ADD if he has six or more symptoms in either or both of these categories. A child can have a) predominantly inattentive type; b) predominantly hyperactive-impulsive type, or c) combined type of ADD. Classroom behavior of the inattentive child is characterized by inattention, distractibility, forgetfulness, failure to follow instructions, daydreaming, and free flight of ideas (internal distractibility). The hyperactive child has the telltale signs of hyperactivity and fidgeting. Both types have poor and inconsistent classroom performance.

ADD should be diagnosed only if the symptoms of inattention and distractibilty are a) considerably more frequent than in most children of the same age and intelligence, b) result in dysfunction at home and school, and c) have lasted more than six months. One should be cautious in diagnosing ADD in two-year-olds, because two-year-olds are generally inattentive and hyperactive. If a child is able to do his schoolwork and chores, gets along with his siblings and peers, and is doing well academically, ADD should not be diagnosed. ADD should be considered only if the child's behavior is affecting his social relations.

The criterion that symptoms should have lasted, in the absence of any stressor, for at least six months ensures that inattention, distractibility, and fidgetiness that occur as a reaction to stressful life events—such as divorce and death—are not mistakenly diagnosed to constitute ADD. The symptoms caused by stressful life events resolve within six months of the onset of the stressful event unless the stressor is chronic. In chronically stressful conditions—such as parental alcoholism and domestic violence—inattention and agitation may last as long as the stressor lasts.

Symptoms of ADD generally manifest before the age of seven years. Even if ADD is first suspected and diagnosed when a child is eight years old, his parents will recall on questioning that the child was difficult, colicky, and fussy as an infant and was terrible at the age of two, having frequent temper tantrums. In fact, if the parents do not recall any such symptoms or assert that the child was an easy, quiet, and cheerful infant, other causes should be explored.

The symptoms of ADD should be present in at least two settings—for example, school and home—to make the diagnosis. If the symptoms of ADD occur only in one setting, the possibility of a situational stressor should be considered. A seven-year-old boy was brought to me with complaints of hyperactivity, inattention, and aggression for the past three months. The child had no problem in the school, but was terrorizing the home. His mother had recently taken in a six-month-old boy for foster care. The younger child had HIV infection and took a lot of the mother's attention. He had to be taken to the hospital very frequently. I reassured this mother that her son was reacting to the addition of the foster child to the family and that his symptoms would abate with time and a little counseling.

Similarly, if the symptoms occur with one person, an interpersonal conflict with that person should be considered. A girl behaved well at home and in most of her classes at school, but acted up in her math class. The mother constantly received notes from that teacher, whereas no one else complained about her daughter. The mother found out that this math teacher was an older woman who commuted daily from New Jersey to New York City. She could not handle so many children in the classroom and had very high expectations of her students. This teacher was having problems with other children, as well.

Diagnosis of ADD should not be made by a physician solely on the basis of his observations of the child in his office, because a clinic is an unnatural setting for a child, where he may not show his true colors. Observations in the office, however, can be used to corroborate parents' and teachers' reports. Similarly, a psychiatric consultation to confirm the diagnosis of ADD is worthless unless it is backed up by the questionnaires. To gather behavioral data objectively, many questionnaires have been developed by psychologists. These questionnaires are first tested (or standardized) on a known population of individuals with ADD, to determine the threshold above which ADD should be diagnosed. The questionnaires often include information about other aspects of a child's behavior as well. Structured questionnaires—such as, Conners parent and teacher questionnaires, Yale children's inventory, and ADD-H Comprehensive Teacher Rating Scale (ACTeRS)—provide more reliable information than the traditional medical interview, because every parent is not a good historian and a parent's perception of his or her child on the day of the interview is often biased by his or her child's behavior on that day. The questionnaires, on the other hand, are filled out by parents and teachers when they are not angry or frustrated, and summarize their observations of the child over a certain period of time.

Once ADD has been diagnosed, the strengths and weaknesses of the child should be identified for the purpose of treatment. The diagnosis of ADD should be open-ended and should be dropped if a child evolves and matures with time. The ADD label should have the sole purpose of helping the child, not to disparage him or her. Labeling should not be stigmatizing; and, last but not least, labeling should not decrease expectations—only make them realistic. Unfortunately, school committees on special education use the label "emotionally disturbed" or "other health impaired" for children with ADD because there is a congressional ban on determining eligibility for special education on the basis of ADD. The term "emotionally disturbed" is confusing as well as demeaning, because the cause of ADD is altered brain chemistry and not psychic conflict.

SUMMARY

Consult a professional if you or your child's teacher suspects that your child has ADD. Many schoolteachers are familiar with ADD questionnaires and often use these to support their suspicion. However, the questionnaire should not be used to make a definitive diagnosis. It should serve as a beacon to seek professional help. A professional familiar with the questionnaires by virtue of training in ADD should review and score them and then make the diagnosis of ADD after carefully excluding other possibilities. A detailed medical, developmental, behavioral, and psychosocial history should be obtained, along with a good physical and neurological examination, to rule out any treatable medical condition, to identify stressors and other diseases that may masquerade as ADD, and to determine secondary complications and coexisting conditions. Secondary complications of ADD are shown schematically in Figure 4 (below). The child's, as well as the parent's, abilities and strengths should also be identified. Parenting capacity and style should also be assessed. This will help in identifying children spoiled by ineffective and inconsistent parenting and in tailoring the parenting style to the needs of the child.

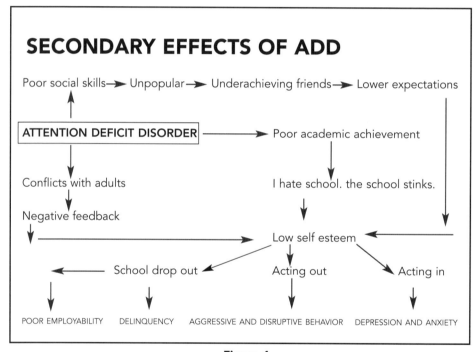

Figure 4

"To intrude, obtrude, impose (upon); to sponge, live at other people's expense; to arrive uninvited or at an inconvenient time, disturb, intrude; to be obtrusive."

[Definition of tfl, the root of the tifl, the word for "child" in the Wehr Dictionary of Arabic.]

JONATHAN RABAN
Arabia, A Journey Through the Labyrinth

10

Is ADD Only a Question of Difficult/Different Temperament?

All children are born different. Some are naturally more active and intrusive than others, some whine at the slightest inconvenience, and some lie contentedly in their cribs. At some stage during their development, most children are active, inattentive, and intrusive. Some mature earlier than others, and some continue to fidget, intrude, and whine long past infant and toddler years. Therefore, is ADD just a question of being different?

According to doctors Stella Chess and Alexander Thomas, each infant is born with a unique, innate temperament. The temperament of an infant is his or her natural style of responding to his or her environment. After following many children for many years in their famous *New York Longitudinal Study*, they described three types of infants—"easy," "slow-to-warm-up," and "difficult"—based upon eight characteristics:

- Physical activity;
- Regularity of physiologic functions, such as hunger, sleep, and elimination;
- Approach to new people, situations, places, and things;
- Adaptability to new situations;

- Intensity or energy level of responses;
- Mood or the amount of pleasant and friendly behavior in various situations;
- Persistence and attention span (the length of time particular activities are pursued by the child with or without obstacles) and distractibility (the effectiveness of extraneous stimuli in interfering with ongoing behaviors);
- Sensory threshold (the amount of stimulation, such as sounds or light, necessary to evoke discernable responses in the child).

A temperamentally difficult child tends to be active, restless, and demanding. While an easy child has regular bowel movements, feeds at scheduled times, and sleeps through the night a few months after birth, a difficult child is irregular in his habits, fussing for food at irregular intervals, including at night. Whereas an easy child is able to tolerate external stimuli better, a difficult child has low sensory threshold and reacts quickly and strongly to even the slightest touch, sound, and light. A difficult child is easily distracted, while the easy child can engage in a pleasant activity without being distracted. An easy child behaves pleasantly most of the time, while a difficult child behaves negatively. A difficult child cannot easily adapt to new situations, while an easy child reacts positively to new situations. The difficult child is inflexible, fusses during transitions, and protests very loudly at the slightest change in routine. A difficult child is not persistent, while an easy child can engage himself or herself in a particular activity without being distracted. For example, an easy child will play with his toes or his hands, while the difficult child will fuss anytime he is left alone. William Carey, a professor of pediatrics at Children's Hospital of Philadelphia, has compiled a parent questionnaire to assess the temperament of children at various ages.

One way to resolve the disease or difficult temperament dilemma is by the concept of *goodness of fit* (or psychosocial homeostasis). According to Drs. Chess and Thomas, most behavioral problems in children occur because of the lack of—or poorness of—fit between the child's temperament and his environment, which includes his parents, siblings, teachers, and peers. Goodness of fit results when the properties of the environment and its expectations and demands are in accord with the child's own capacities, motivations, and style of behavior. When this consonance is present, the child's behavior is simply a developmental variation and optimal development is possible. Information obtained on the temperament questionnaire can be used by parents to adapt their child-rearing style to the temperament of the child, to obtain goodness of fit. When this goodness of fit is not obtained and dissonance and conflict are present, a disorder exists.

The concept of temperament does not invalidate ADD as a disease entity. On the contrary, it supports the argument that ADD is a constitutionally— perhaps genetically—predetermined condition that results in a very intense and highly active and reactive temperament that results in dis-ease or dis-adaptation. Temperament is assumed to be the biologically based, emotional core of personality.

The range of human behavior is so wide that almost every symptom of a disease can occasionally occur in a person who does not have that disease. For example, headaches can occur in both healthy people and in those with brain tumors. A healthy person can occasionally be suspicious of others' motives, but a similar feeling is also a valid symptom of paranoid schizophrenia. It is the intensity and pervasiveness of a symptom, and resulting dysfunction and disease that establish a disease, not the mere presence of the symptom. Inattention, distractibility, impulsivity, and hyperactivity can occur in normal children, but they suggest a disorder only when these symptoms put a child and his family at dis-ease.

The concept of temperament, although scientifically valid, has a practical problem. The children labeled as "difficult" or "easy," may build their self-images around these perceptions and play these out in their lives, fulfilling the prophecy. The parents of a so-called difficult child may accept and rationalize negative behaviors of their child as inevitable instead of rectifying them, further worsening his behavior. In the process of adapting their child-rearing style to their child's temperament, they may compromise rules of their family and decrease their expectations of their child. Even if parents were to alter their parenting style, it is utopian to expect that teachers would be able to adapt their teaching style to the temperament of each of their pupils.

Delaying treatment of children whose symptoms far exceed the threshold of normality can result in secondary complications. The temperament of a child is only as bad or as good as the way his parents perceive it; and what is easy for one parent, may be difficult for the other parent. The responsibility of treating a child mainly by adapting their child-rearing style to the temperament of their child is an onerous one for the parents. Parents vary in their skills and life situations and may not be ready to take on the responsibility of becoming their child's therapist.

Although the concept of innate nature and constitution is fascinating, it is difficult to measure. As many as 18,000 personality traits—including traits troublesome to others (anger, envy, bitterness), traits troublesome to self (ambivalence and over-sensitivity), and positive traits (joviality, serenity, assertiveness, and honesty)—have been described by psychologists. Comprehensive description of a child's personality would require a series of costly and prolonged evaluations by a number of professionals—such as psychologists, educational specialists, and neuropsychiatrists—and is not feasible. Such evaluations are not paid for by insurers because they require medical diagnosis instead of narrative descriptions. Various professionals will not be able to communicate easily with one another through these unwieldy narratives.

Therefore, it is more practical to diagnose a child with suggestive symptoms as having attention deficit disorder, rather than difficult temperament. Once this is done, the strengths and weaknesses of a child can be assessed and one can work to remedy his weaknesses and build on his strengths.

11

Can Parents and Teachers Diagnose ADD By Using Questionnaires?

Although questionnaires are used to confirm the diagnosis of ADD and to monitor the effects of medications, the range of possible problems in a child with ADD is too broad to be captured by a questionnaire alone. Many medical and mental conditions—such as depression, anxiety, stress, bipolar disorder, juvenile mania, and posttraumatic stress disorder—can masquerade as ADD and are likely to be missed by a cookbook approach to the diagnosis of ADD. Although parents can certainly suspect that something is wrong with their child, they often lack the objectivity that a professional brings to the diagnosis. Although a teacher's input is certainly very valuable, a teacher is usually not privy to all the information about the family that is required to make a definite diagnosis. Therefore, the diagnosis of ADD should be made by a professional who specializes in the diagnosis and management of children with behavior problems, after obtaining information from multiple sources, examining the child, and carefully considering all the conditions that can cause symptoms similar to ADD (see Chapter 14 on differential diagnosis: "Does Everyone Who Moves Have ADD?").

Similarly, a physician should not diagnose ADD solely on the basis of a critical score in a questionnaire. Medicine is called an art, not a science, because the physician, like an artist, looks at the whole picture—the gestalt—and makes a mental impression. This is especially true in behavioral disorders. Although the American Psychiatric Association has done a great job by bringing some sanity to the madness by grouping symptoms into disorders, *DSM-IV* criteria alone should not be used to diagnose disorders. One should look at the child, the family, the school, the peers, the siblings, and the frequency, intensity, and pervasiveness of symptoms, as well as the dysfunction and distress that the symptoms are causing.

The debate about the role of teachers in diagnosing ADD has been galvanized recently by a Colorado Board of Education ruling that discourages teachers from recommending behavioral drugs, such as Ritalin and Luvox, for children. Although the reasoning behind this ruling—psychotropic medications cause violent behavior— is faulty, it underscores that teachers should not be in the business of diagnosing medical disorders and giving medical advice, and should not bring undue pressure upon parents and physicians to prescribe medications for children with behavioral problems. However, teachers play a key role in the diagnosis and management of ADD by suspecting that something is wrong with a child, bringing it to the notice of the parents and physicians, monitoring response to medications, and implementing behavioral strategies.

12

Can ADD Occur with Other Disorders?

Disorders and diseases do not come in cookie-cutter shapes as the books would have us believe. They occur as mix-and-match, in unique combinations of symptoms, signs, problems, and complications. ADD is no exception: as many as thirty-to-forty percent of children who have ADD also have associated disorders (*comorbid disorders*) and complications that make their presentation unique (Figure 5).

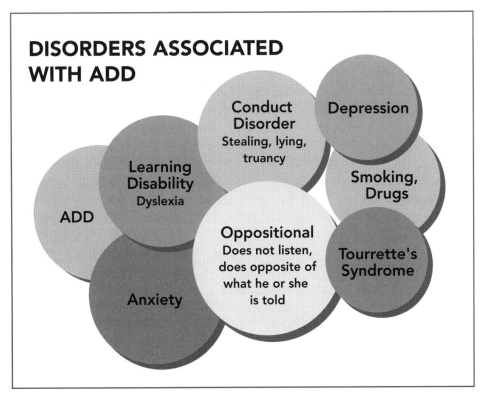

DISORDERS ASSOCIATED WITH ADD

Conduct Disorder
Stealing, lying, truancy

Depression

Learning Disability
Dyslexia

Smoking, Drugs

ADD

Oppositional
Does not listen, does opposite of what he or she is told

Anxiety

Tourrette's Syndrome

Figure 5

Learning disability (LD): Learning disability (also called *different learning style or learning inability*) is defined as the inability to read, spell, write, or compute at age and grade level despite normal intelligence, normal vision and hearing, and adequate educational opportunities. Imagine two persons who have to go from Harlem to Wall Street in New York City. One has a Lexus (higher horsepower or intelligence) and the other has a Toyota Tercel. The one who has the Lexus does not know the best route and does not know how to negotiate the streets of Manhattan (neuropsychological processes), whereas the other is a pro in negotiating the roads and traffic of Manhattan. The first person will not be able to reach his destination (achieve his goal) despite his more powerful automobile (higher intelligence), and is thus analogous to a person with LD. Children with LD cannot perform the processes involved in learning—listening, interpreting and storing incoming information, and retrieving already-stored information. LD is believed to occur due to faulty circuitry in areas of the brain that are involved in the neuropsychological processing of information and memory. Dyslexia—or the inability to read—is the most common type of learning disability.

As many as forty percent of children with ADD have LD, as well. LD not only co-exists with ADD, but also raises the chicken-and-egg issue: is a child inattentive because he does not understand what is going on in the classroom, or does he not understand what is going on in the classroom because he is inattentive? This is not a rhetorical question, but a practical one. The grades of a child with primary disorder of attention may improve significantly after psychostimulant medication is administered. A child with LD, on the other hand, will not improve significantly until he receives special education. Sometimes the distinction may not be so clear-cut, and it is more useful to find the strengths and weaknesses of the child instead of categorically classifying him as learning disabled or inattentive.

Children who have both ADD and LD are at a very high risk for school failure and poor employability.

Conduct disorder or maladaptive behavior: About ten-to-fifteen percent of children with ADD may have severe behavior problems, such as setting fires, hitting and hurting others, cruelty to animals, stealing, lying, and truancy. These behaviors are considered to be the signs of a severe psychiatric condition called conduct disorder. Children with conduct disorder, characteristically, have no remorse for their actions and pose a danger to others. Children with conduct disorder should be managed by psychiatrists.

Oppositional behavior: An oppositional child does not listen to his parents and does not do what they tell him to do. In fact, he may do exactly the opposite of what his parents tell him to do, as the term *oppositional* suggests. Parents complain that their child is disobedient, disrespectful, and noncompliant. Such behavior may be a complication of ADD itself, as described before, or may be a reflection of an underlying emotional problem, such as, anxiety, depression, or a conflict between child and parents. As many as forty percent of the children in the Multimodal Treatment Study conducted by the National Institute of Mental Health met the criteria for oppositional disorder. Children with oppositional disorder should be seen by a psychiatrist.

Anxiety and depression (disorders of mood): Anxiety occurs both as a coexisting condition and as a complication of ADD. Thirty-four percent of children in the Multimodal Treatment Study were diagnosed to have an anxiety disorder. Children with ADD, especially adolescents, may be anxious and depressed because they realize that they are different from other children and may not be able to meet the challenges of independent living that school and workplace demand.

Tourette's syndrome: This disease is characterized by involuntary tics, such as grimacing, hiccupping, speaking obscenities, and clearing the throat. Many children with Tourette's have obsessive-compulsive disorder as well. Obsessive-compulsive disorder involves compulsions—or an irresistible tendency to repeat the same acts again and again, such as washing hands and turning electric switches off and on. Obsessive-compulsive disorder (OCD), Tourette's syndrome, and ADD often run in families, with one child having Tourette's and another obsessive-compulsive disorder.

Complications of ADD: Low self-esteem and poor academic achievement are the most important consequences of ADD. One of the primary motivations for human behavior is to win approval by the most important person (object) in one's life, such as, a mother, father, teacher, or peer. Children with ADD are thwarted in their efforts to win this approval, resulting in maladaptive defenses to protect their self-identity or ego.

They may act silly like clowns and deny that they have any problem, or project their inadequacy onto their parents, blaming them for their failures. They project their own misdeeds onto their peers in school: "They are all mean to me." They displace their anger onto authority figures, their weaker peers, or their younger siblings.

Due to persistent negative feedback from the people dearest to them, they develop a negative image of themselves—an "I am not OK" image—in their own minds: "I am messed up," "I am screwed up," or "I am f….d up." Even if they behave well and others compliment them, they doubt that they behaved well, feeling that the others are either complimenting them just out of love or are manipulating them with an ulterior motive. They feel that everyone is out to get them, and, driven by this feeling of persecution, they often strike at others preemptively.

Many children with ADD get poorer grades, repeat grades, and are assigned to special classes. Poor academic achievement despite normal intelligence is very frustrating to parents and children alike and leads to children's poor self-esteem and negative attitude toward learning in children. A child may find schoolwork very cumbersome and may give up, spending time watching MTV or just hanging out. Hanging out on street corners with other underachieving children is like being in "Fagin's* workshop," because smoking, sexual activity, marijuana, and cocaine often begin on street corners. Peers have a tremendous effect on children with low self-esteem making them feel at home and accepted. Peers provide an outlet against the establishment, a place to get even with those who failed and faulted the child.

A few children do not accept that they are different or not up to snuff. Instead of working on their disability, such children may rebel against their parents and society, asking, "Why me?" A few children hate being labeled; and others hate being pulled out of their classes to go to the nurse to take medicine in the middle of the day.

Children with low self-esteem and those who have a poor attitude toward learning may benefit from counseling, psychotherapy, and special education. Every child is different and reacts differently to his condition. Similarly, every parent is different in his or her response. Therefore, there can be no cookbook approach to treatment.

---

* Fagin, a villain in *Oliver Twist* by Charles Dickens, teaches orphans to perform acts of villainy.

"Seek, and ye shall find; knock, and it shall be opened unto you."

NEW TESTAMENT, MATT. 7:7

13

Is There a Litmus Test for ADD?

Although the diagnostic approach in conventional western medicine is summed up in the above quote from the New Testament, ADD belies it because, despite the amazing advances in medical technology that have been made in the past century, no tool or test of neurology or psychology can diagnose ADD or find its cause with certainty. A few of these tests are discussed below so that parents can make an informed choice about whether a particular test is required for their child or not.

Electroencephalogram (EEG): The brain cells communicate with one another electrically and chemically. The electrical activity of the brain can be recorded on paper through electrodes attached to the front (medically called frontal leads), middle (temporal leads), and the back (occipital leads) of the skull. The resulting tracing, often recorded on reams and reams of paper, is called EEG. A neurologist then looks at the tracing for abnormalities. The waveforms are classified as alpha, beta, theta, and delta, depending upon their rate and height. Although an excess of theta (slow waves) and shortage of beta waves (fast waves) in the frontal area of the brain have been described in a few individuals with ADD, the finding is not consistent enough to be of diagnostic value in ADD. Automated recording and analysis of electric activity of the brain with computer-generated colored maps of the brain have also been problematic because of artifacts and the difficulty of separating the chance findings from real ones.

Computerized axial tomography (CAT or CT scan) of the head: CAT (the acronym CT is also used) scan of the head consists of computer-generated images of the brain in various planes produced after the child's head is exposed to x-rays. Irradiation is similar to that involved in a plain film of the skull. CT scan of the brain is a good test to identify problems with the structure of the brain—such as bleeding, calcification, enlargement of the ventricles (conduits and cisterns through which the cerebral fluid flows), and tumor—but does not provide any information about the function of the brain. Although inattention and hyperactivity can be minor symptoms of a few of these conditions, it is unlikely that no other symptoms would be present. For example, children with a condition called hydrocephalus (enlarged cerebral fluid cisterns and pathways) sometimes appear to have ADD because they talk garrulously, but it is very unlikely that they would not have more ominous symptoms of hydrocephalus— such as headache, increased reflexes, wobbly gait, and blurred vision. A CAT scan of the head will certainly be indicated in the latter scenario, but there is no indication for obtaining this costly investigation in a child who does not have symptoms other than inattention and hyperactivity.

Magnetic resonance imaging (MRI), or nuclear magnetic resonance (NMR): This is another popular tool for investigation that is considered by some to be the mother of all diagnostic tests for the disorders of the human brain. This test is based upon the fact that every atom has magnetic properties. The MRI harnesses the magnetic properties of hydrogen atoms to produce pictures of the brain without using x-rays. The child is put inside a huge person-sized tube with a strong magnetic field. Radio frequency waves are created when hydrogen atoms, acting as tiny magnets, move in this magnetic field. These waves, when analyzed by the computer, give accurate and detailed pictures of the brain. No radiation is involved. Like CAT scan, MRI gives useful information on the structure of the brain; but ADD is due to neurotransmitter dysfunction, which cannot be detected by MRI. The procedure is time-consuming and costly. Although better techniques are being developed, in which the child does not have to go inside a tube, most children have to be given a sedative so that they do not move and are not terrified of the equipment and the personnel operating it. The benefits of the procedure are so minuscule in cases of ADD—if there are any at all—that the cost is not worth it.

If a neurologist refers you for MRI, ask him or her what he or she expects to see in the MRI based upon this examination. Has he or she seen signs of a disease of the brain that is likely to be detected by MRI? Will MRI help in choosing a particular type of therapy, or surgery. Prognosis alone is not enough of an indication, because predictions based upon minor anomalies may not be accurate and can become self-fulfilling prophecies. Do not accept an investigation if the doctor tells you that he or she just wants to find out what is going on in the brain.

Positron emission tomography scan (PET): Positron-emitting radioactive isotopes, produced in a cyclotron, are incorporated into a biologically active substance, such as glucose, that is then injected into the body. Tomographic images (sliced images) of the brain are generated by the computer, based upon the concentration of the radioactive tracer in the brain. The procedure is used to study the blood flow in the brain and uptake of oxygen by the various tissues, as well as to assess utilization of glucose by different areas of the brain. This is not a clinically useful tool for ADD because of a high possibility of false negative results and prohibitive cost.

Single photon emission computerized tomography (SPECT): This technique involves the injection of a small dose of a radioactive substance— Xenon-133—to examine the blood flow in different areas of the brain. In individuals with ADD, researchers have reported poor blood flow in the areas of the brain involved in attention (frontal lobes and caudate nucleus, a collection of brain cells buried deep in the brain) and increased blood flow in the areas of the brain that are involved in receiving sensory information and responding to it (the sensory and sensorimotor cortex). However, many children with ADD may not show any abnormalities in this test (false negatives), while a few children without ADD may have misleading positive findings (false positives). Although the test is cheaper than PET, the pictures obtained are of poorer quality.

Recently, a group of researchers found a characteristic pattern on SPECT in six adults with ADD, when they used radioactively-tagged Altropane, a substance that binds selectively to dopamine transporter protein, raising the possibility of diagnostic test for ADD. However, the media hype about this test was premature because the test was done on only six individuals. It will have to go through rigorous scrutiny by scientific and regulatory agencies before it hits the market.

Continuous performance tests (CPT): Children are presented with rapidly moving letters on a computer screen or on a video screen. They are told to respond to all letters except when a particular sequence occurs. For example, in the version sold by Dr. C. Keith Conners (Conners' Continuous Performance Test), the child is supposed to hit the keyboard space bar any time he sees a letter on the screen except when an X follows an A. The computer software then generates a number of measures that are used to assess inattention: errors of omission, slow reaction time, inconsistency of responses, and change in reaction time over time. Impulsivity is suggested by errors of commission and quick response. (Three CPTs are available in the marketplace: Gordon's diagnostic system, Conners' CPT, and TOVA—Test of Vigilance and Attention.)

A CPT is not essential for the diagnosis of ADD. It does not assess a child under natural conditions; and therefore often results in misdiagnosis. The results depend upon a child's motivation and facility with computers. However, a few clinicians find it useful to monitor the effects of medications.

Freedom from distractibility factor (FFD) in WISC: Weschler Intelligence Scale for Children is the most commonly used test to measure the intelligence of children. Arithmetic, coding, and digit span tasks (subtests) on this test require the child to reflect and pay attention. The psychologist calculates a score called *freedom from distractibility (FFD)* score based upon the child's performance in these subtests. This score is not diagnostic by itself, but can be used to help to support findings from other sources. If the scores are consistently low in these three subtests of FFD, and if there is a wide discrepancy between the scores in subtests of this factor and the subtests of the two other factors of WISC—the verbal comprehension and spatial organization factors—there is greater likelihood of ADD.

Measures of activity: Activity of a child can be measured by using special cushions, self-winding watches, and actometers. The problem with activity measures is that the child can be active for a variety of reasons other than ADD. Unless parents maintain an accurate diary of all the activities of the child when he or she is hooked to the device, the test is unlikely to yield valid results. There is a very high rate of false positives. Additionally, these devices are costly. Manufacturers charge exorbitant fees to loan these devices and to decode and interpret the results.

Structured observations in classroom or laboratory: On-task and off-task behavior is measured by an expert directly or by videotaping. It is a time- and labor-intensive method. Imagine a physician spending two to three hours observing the child in the child's school. Who would pay for it? Similarly, videotaping in a classroom will entail obtaining informed consents from parents of other the children in the classroom and from the teacher's union.

SUMMARY

Many of the tests that have been used to study the phenomenon of ADD in groups do not fair well with individual patients. They identify children who do not have ADD (false positive) or fail to identify those who have ADD (false negative). Because they study children in laboratories rather than in their natural environments, they do not capture the children's natural behavior. And, last but not least, they examine these children at only one or two points of time—rather than over a prolonged period of time—to assess the inability of children with ADD to sustain effort over time.

"ADD is a seductive diagnosis. We have to be very careful not to overdiagnose ADD."

EDWARD HALLOWELL, MD

14

Does Everyone Who Moves Have ADD?
DIFFERENTIAL DIAGNOSIS

The symptoms of hyperactivity and inattention do not occur exclusively in ADD. They can occur in typical children when they are excited or under stress. They occur in other psychiatric disorders, such as anxiety and depression, as well. All these conditions must be considered and excluded before one arrives at the diagnosis of ADD. This process of sifting the chaff from the grain—called *differential diagnosis*—is time-consuming and should be done by an experienced clinician specializing in ADD.

Differential diagnosis involves obtaining medical, developmental, and social information about the child and the family by interview and questionnaires, performing a thorough medical and neurological examination, assessing the mental status of the child, and ordering and reviewing laboratory tests. This process cannot be completed in a fifteen-minute visit to a doctor, but requires two or more visits of forty-five minutes to one hour each. A rush to diagnose ADD in a quick-fix approach to the symptoms of hyperactivity and inattention may hide some of the psychiatric and social conditions described below, with serious consequences.

Dysfunctional family (inadequate, disorganized, and chaotic home): David, a three-year-old, is referred to the clinic to rule out ADD. His mother is a thin-built—almost emaciated—white woman in her twenties, dressed in shabby clothes and poorly groomed. She is very distrustful of the nurses, doctors, teachers, and the world at large. She starts off the visit by rattling off the negative qualities of people around her, including her child: "He is always running around. I have to constantly supervise him. I can't work or go to school because he wouldn't stay still. He is such a brat." The child has a flat facial expression, but walks to the dollhouse and starts exploring the doll. The mother runs after him, allegedly fearful that he will fall and hurt himself. She talks incessantly, trying to correct and teach the boy. The child appears to be under siege. History reveals that this young woman has been on the streets since the age of sixteen. She grew up in New Jersey until the age of thirteen, when she was taken by her grandparents to Ohio after both her parents died in a car crash. She ran away from her grandparents' house, returned to the tri-state area, and has been in one shelter after another since then. She is not sure who the child's father is—she met him in a shelter. It appears from her demeanor that she has a mental disorder, although she denies having seen a psychiatrist and is very upset at the insinuation of a psychiatric disorder. "What has my condition to do with my child? I have come to see you for the child and not for myself."

According to social scientist Albert Bandura, a child learns by imitating actions of others around him. In this situation, the child saw only chaos and that is all he learned. He did not know better. There was nothing for him to pay attention to. Children learn to behave from their parents, siblings, and peers. If their parents are disorganized, inconsistent, and careless, children may learn to be disorganized, inconsistent, and careless. Although ADD is not caused by dysfunctional parenting, living in such chaotic conditions as David lives in can disturb environmental and mental homeostasis in a child predisposed to behavioral dysregulation. Therefore, it is essential that parents put their own house in order before they consider ADD in their children. Similarly, before a physician makes the diagnosis of ADD, he should explore the family environment and the parenting capacity of the parents.

A psychiatric disorder in parents—especially maternal depression—affects parent/child relations negatively. A depressed mother sees everything around her, including her children, negatively. So if Johnny gets B's in one marking period, she concludes that Johnny will not be promoted, and starts brooding and worrying about it. If Johnny replies to her a little firmly, she thinks that Johnny is being disrespectful and rebellious. She behaves erratically with her children depending upon her mood swings. She showers them with undeserved rewards when she feels good and scolds them unnecessarily when she is blue, sending them confused messages. Parents with a psychiatric disease may be so preoccupied with or impaired by their own condition that they may not interact with their children emotionally and physically. Therefore, parents should always examine their own feelings to see if they are not making their child a target of their own frustrations and failures. They should certainly not become defensive when a clinician points this out to them.

Poorness of fit: Before diagnosing ADD, one should also exclude mismatch— or, in the words of the famous psychiatrists Stella Chess and Alexander Thomas, *poorness of fit* between the child's temperament and environmental demands. For example, taciturn, puritanical parents who like classical music may think that their loquacious, noisy son who prefers rap and reggae has ADD. Similarly, a near-retirement suburban teacher may consider a hip-hop, inner-city teen to have ADD. Social conflicts resulting from such mismatch can masquerade as ADD.

Mental retardation: Individuals with low IQ may have decreased ability to initiate and sustain attention and may be hyperactive. A ten-year-old child with an IQ of thirty is likely to behave like a three-year-old child with poor attention span and impulsivity characteristic of a three-year-old. Children with mental retardation may not be able to think of the consequences of their actions and may by impulsive. However, it is usually not difficult to differentiate children with severe forms of mental retardation from those with ADD, because the former are delayed in achieving their developmental milestones—they learn to walk and talk late and may not be able to perform activities of daily living, such as learning to brush their teeth or put on their clothes. The milder forms of mental retardation are sometimes not identified until early elementary grades and may be confused with ADD.

Pervasive developmental disorder and autism: Children with autism can be agitated, hyperactive, and inattentive at one end of the spectrum and overfocused on a single aspect of their environment at the other. Children with autism do not establish eye contact, they do not respond to their names, and either do not talk at all or repeat whatever others say verbatim. Whereas it is not difficult to identify a typically autistic child, a child with a milder form of autism— euphemistically called pervasive developmental disorder—can sometimes be considered a hyperactive child.

Anxiety and depression (mood disorders): Both anxiety and depression can cause inattention and hyperactivity. Many people get butterflies in their stomach, pace up and down the room, and frenetically cross and open their legs before an interview or an examination. A child whose parents fight like cats and dogs and threaten to kill each other every night is unlikely to pay attention in the classroom. A child who is worrying about his family being thrown out on the street for defaulting on the rent is unlikely to pay attention to the teacher, as well. Children with anxiety may bite their nails and pull their hair out, may have nightmares, and may panic in some situations. Children with depression may not eat or sleep well and may like to stay aloof. They may lose interest in activities that they previously liked. They may either not do anything or may move from one activity to another without completing anything. They may be slow or agitated. Whereas symptoms of ADD surface in early childhood, depression occurs later in childhood and is particularly common among adolescents.

Mania phase of bipolar disorder and unipolar mania: Bipolar disorder is a serious disorder of mood in which the child vacillates between periods of euphoria and depression. The mania phase of bipolar disorder may present itself as ADD. Such individuals act grandiosely, taking dangerous risks. They are restless and agitated and talk incessantly. They are easily distracted and cannot focus. They sleep for a few hours and then appear to have boundless energy. A child with juvenile mania may jump from the rooftop, believing that he is Superman. This disorder should be managed by a psychiatrist. Medications such as Ritalin may be harmful in such cases.

Speech and language disorder: If a child is not able to understand what her parents are saying to her, she is likely to be inattentive, and confused, and act out her frustrations. Similarly, auditory integration problems can present themselves as inattention because the child cannot integrate information coming through both his ears or fails to process certain sound frequencies. Imagine that you have to listen to two radio stations simultaneously: 100.3 FM and 1010 WINS. Or that you hear "Oh, my Dog" instead of "Oh, my God."

If a child has speech and language problems, he should be evaluated and treated by an audiologist for his hearing and then by a speech pathologist to rule out a language disorder or auditory integration problem, before ADD is diagnosed. However, in a few cases, language delay can be the cart and not the horse, because attention is a prerequisite for learning language as well. If a child does not attend to the sounds in his environment, he will not learn to speak. Once again, a trained clinician or a team of clinicians is required to make this distinction.

Adjustment disorder (stressed child): Children often respond to stressors—such as, parental separation, death of a parent, witnessing violence, change of school, and loss of a pet—with inattention and deteriorating school performance.

A ten-year-old girl was referred to me to be evaluated for ADD. Her teachers had observed that she was often "spaced out" in her class and did not seem to listen. Her grades had fallen. On examination, this girl appeared rather sad but complied with all requests and did not appear inattentive. In the picture she drew of her family, she was standing with outstretched hands between her parents who stood facing in opposite directions. Her three wishes were that her parents lived together, her dead hamster would come back to life, and she could talk to her grandmother who had died a year ago. On questioning, I found out that her parents were in the process of divorce and this girl was trying her best to bring them together. She did not have ADD, but she was reacting to multiple losses in her life.

A twelve-year-old boy with HIV-1 infection was referred to me to rule out ADD. He did not have any diseases related to his HIV-1 infection and was growing and developing well. Since the age of ten months, he had been in the care of his maternal aunt who had an intact family with two other children. On questioning, the boy verbalized that he worried about his health and whether he would be able to go to the school when he fell sick. He had not been told that his mother died of AIDS, but he often fantasized about it. Although he met the *DSM* criteria for the inattentive type of ADD, I referred him to a psychologist to deal with his anxiety.

Spoiled child (brat): A twenty-four-year-old single mother and her seven-year-old son were referred to me by the child's schoolteachers. The teacher wrote, "He cannot stay still in the classroom, does not listen, fights with other children, and tries to hit the teacher when asked to stay in his seat." His mother was very angry with his teachers, alleging that there was nothing wrong with her son and that the teachers were racists. She continued to rant and rave while her son ravaged my office. He touched every gadget, from the otoscope to the garbage can. His mother did not ask him even once to stay still or not to touch things without permission. He constantly interrupted us, first verbally and then by pulling at his mother's blouse. She had no idea what disciplining meant. This was her only child, they slept in the same bed, and she took him wherever she went. She bought him anything he asked for. He literally ran her life.

Another vignette: a father who showered boundless love upon his only daughter when he came home from work. He reprimanded his wife in front of the child if she asked the child not to jump on the bed or not to make noise. The child complained about her mother to the father, and he argued with the mother about it. He grudgingly accompanied his wife to my office, but constantly denied that anything was wrong with his daughter, while his wife complained and cried.

Another spoiled-child scenario is of two grandparents who pampered their grandson and constantly chided the parents for disciplining him, thus undermining the parents' authority.

Spoiling can also occur if a child who, because his parents died in an accident or of sickness, is being raised by a relative who, out of pity, does not set limits:

> "He's my own dead sister's boy, poor thing, and I ain't got the heart to lash him, somehow. Every time I let him off, my conscience does hurt me so, and every time I hit him my old heart breaks."
> Aunt Polly, *The Adventures of Tom Sawyer*.

Some parents do not set limits, because they are afraid that the child is too fragile to withstand the negative (often imagined) effects of his outbursts. Premature children and children with chronic medical conditions—such as asthma, congenital heart defect, and epilepsy—are particularly prone to spoiling. Children in families with a history of death of a previous child are also susceptible to spoiling. Spoiling can be cultural as well. In an Asian-Indian family, the only son born after three daughters is likely to be raised as a prince, with no limits.

Attention seeking versus attention deficit: Too much love is as bad as too little love. A few children become so addicted to attention and praise that they do not comply until a bribe is promised. They may interrupt you first verbally and then physically until you acknowledge them and reaffirm that they did something right. They may act like clowns to draw attention to themselves. Children with low self-esteem often seek attention as a reassurance of their self-worth.

Disorders of short-term memory: Children with a deficit of short-term memory often forget instructions, appear oppositional, seem inattentive.

Children with deficits in active working memory cannot keep pace with schoolwork and tune out. Using the terminology of computers, the latter do not have enough random-access memory (RAM) and crash when input exceeds RAM.

Disorders of sequential processing: The human brain has the ability to keep a series of words and instructions in a proper sequence and hold them in active working memory until it can process them and decide what to do with them. Children with deficits in sequential processing tend to get confused when a series of instructions is given to them. They appear inattentive or oppositional.

Disorders of central auditory processing: Children with auditory processing problems have difficulty in understanding speech under poor acoustic conditions, because they cannot distinguish speech from background noise. They have a difficult time understanding other people in uncarpeted hallways, in shopping malls, when they are seated near a window when road work is going on outside, and when people speak from another room. They also have difficulty in understanding people who speak rapidly, have an unfamiliar accent, or poor pronunciation. In one of these disorders, the brain cannot integrate and interpret the signals coming from the two ears at the same time. It is like being tuned to two radio stations at the same time, each competing with the other for attention of the brain. The message gets garbled and the child appears inattentive and confused. Testing for these disorders is done by specially-trained audiologists.

Sleep disorders: Excessive daytime sleepiness due to inadequate or inefficient sleep at night can cause inattention. This happens in children who have difficulty breathing at night due to enlarged tonsils, falling back of the tongue, or a host of other medical conditions. Adolescents or young adults often go to bed late and get up early for the school, incurring a debt of sleep that results in excessive daytime sleepiness and inattention.

Other medical conditions: Some cold and cough remedies can cause drowsiness in some children and hyperalertness and hyperactivity in others. Phenobarb, a medication for epilepsy, causes hyperactivity in some children. In petit mal—a type of epilepsy—a child momentarily stops doing whatever he or she was doing and appears not to pay attention. Itching due to allergic eczema can also cause agitation and inattention.

15
Does ADD Occur in Girls Too?

Although ADD occurs more frequently in boys than girls (in a ratio between 4:1 and 9:1), girls are by no means immune to this condition. According to the National Ambulatory Medical Survey for the years 1990 through 1995, the number of office-based visits with girls diagnosed with ADD increased 3.9-fold during that five-year period.

In the past, gender-role stereotyping of girls subdued the expression of their innate nature. They were taught to walk gracefully and talk softly, while their brothers were allowed to scream and stomp. They were taught to work with their mothers in the kitchen or play with dolls, while their brothers played ball in the street. Today a girl participates in all the activities a boy does, including baseball and soccer. She can laugh loudly and roughhouse without being admonished for lack of modesty. The hyperactivity and loquaciousness of a girl with ADD expresses itself earlier and freely under such conditions.

Changing societal expectations are contributing to ADD being diagnosed more often in girls today than before. Both boys and girls are expected to go to school and be good students. Parents are as concerned when their daughter does not do well at school as they are when their son does not do well. A search for the causes of failure in school results in ADD being diagnosed early and more often. Although ADD without hyperactivity (inattentive type) has been reported to be more common in girls than in boys, girls and boys with ADD are essentially similar in their presentation. Girls with ADD, however, report more social difficulties than boys.

The prevalence of ADD in girls increases with age. Whereas ADD is more common in boys at younger ages, by adolescence, it is as common in girls as in boys.

Section II

MANAGEMENT OF ADD

16
Who Should Treat ADD?

ADD is a fashionable disease; therefore, professionals from many disciplines—pediatricians, developmental-behavioral pediatricians, psychiatrists, neurologists, psychologists, and social workers—claim to specialize in its treatment. However, none of them can claim a monopoly on this disease. Choosing the right professional depends upon the severity of ADD, coexisting conditions, and secondary complications. For the purpose of management, ADD can be classified as uncomplicated ADD—if there are no coexisting conditions and secondary complications—or as complicated ADD, if there are.

Uncomplicated ADD: If the primary care pediatrician believes that the child has mild ADD without any educational, behavioral, and social complications, he or she should be able to manage the child with periodic input from the parents and schoolteachers. The pediatrician is a logical choice if the child has a treatable medical cause that is causing the symptoms of inattention and hyperactivity. According to a study conducted by the National Institute of Mental Health, most children with ADD in the United States are treated by pediatricians. However, the pediatrician should be familiar with ADD and should be willing to obtain a detailed medical, developmental, and social history; review the questionnaires; and perform physical, neurologic, and developmental examinations. It is more than likely, however, that a pediatrician will not be able to spend the amount of time that management of ADD requires, especially if he has a capitation contract with an HMO. Under a capitation contract, a pediatrician receives a flat monthly reimbursement for a child regardless of the services provided or time spent.

If a child's hyperactivity and inattention are a result of a temporary stressor and pediatric counseling does not resolve it, a clinical social worker or a clinical psychologist may be consulted to support the child and the family through the crisis and its aftermath.

If the pediatrician does not have time and the child has moderate simple (uncomplicated) ADD, the parents should see a *developmental-behavioral pediatrician*. Developmental-behavioral pediatricians are a new breed of pediatric subspecialists who specialize in managing children with disabling developmental and behavioral conditions. They can spend more time in obtaining the history, examine the child more carefully, communicate with the child's school, interpret reports for the parents, separate the chaff from the grain, and decide what further services the child might require. Developmental-behavioral pediatricians are cost-effective because in most cases the buck will stop there. An alternative approach is to begin with a clinical psychologist, but psychologists cannot prescribe medications, the mainstay of ADD treatment.

If neither a developmental-behavioral pediatrician nor a psychologist is available, one can consult a psychiatrist or a neurologist. Any of these routes can be taken depending upon availability and the parents' comfort level.

The above scenario plays out when you have unlimited choices, but choices for treating ADD in managed care are limited and inappropriate. Your health insurance company may leave the decision to the primary care provider (PCP), who may or may not refer you to the limited number of specialists on the HMO's panel of providers. In many cases, the decision may be made, whimsically, based entirely on fiscal considerations by an insurance company employee who knows little about ADD. Therefore, it is imperative for parents to learn more about ADD and its management so that they can obtain the best services for their children.

ADD complicated by other conditions: If a child with ADD has an additional educational or mental health condition or has secondary complications, he should be seen by another specialist, depending on his or her symptoms. Following are a few suggestions in such cases:

• **Poor or failing performance in school:** In such cases, assessment of IQ by a psychologist and educational evaluation by a learning-disabilities specialist (special education teacher) should be done to rule out learning disability. This may be done by the school's child study team (also called the committee on special education) or privately if you do not want the school to be involved. Whereas the psychologist's services are usually reimbursed by third-party payers, educational evaluations are not. There are, however, ways in which the latter can be partly reimbursed. If you do not agree with the school's evaluations, the local board of education can be asked to pay for second opinions, if you so desire. You may have to hire an advocate if the school is unwilling to do so.

• **Severe behavior problems:** If a child is oppositional, aggressive, lies, steals, runs away from school, is anxious, depressed, obsessive-compulsive, or hallucinates (complains that he hears or sees things that do not exist), his mental status should be evaluated by a psychiatrist. Depending on what is diagnosed, ongoing therapy can be provided by a psychiatrist, a clinical psychologist, or a psychiatric social worker. A psychiatrist can provide consultation for medications, whereas a psychologist or a social worker can provide psychotherapy.

• **Tics, headaches, or seizures:** A child with these symptoms should by seen be a neurologist. Tics are involuntary movements of the face and other parts of the body, such as facial grimacing and shrugging of the shoulders.

• **Clumsiness:** A clumsy child should be seen by an occupational therapist to rule out and manage developmental coordination disorder.

• **Problems in speech, language, or auditory processing:** A child with these symptoms should be seen by a speech and language pathologist and a specialist in auditory processing disorder.

SUMMARY
It is not necessary for every child with ADD to see a neurologist, psychiatrist, psychologist, and, certainly not, an occupational therapist. Although a so-called multidisciplinary evaluation by a number of professionals is very popular, it overwhelms the child and labels the child in all possible ways. Multidisciplinary evaluations make already scarce resources unavailable to children who really need them, and provide them to those who do not need them. Therefore, evaluations should be symptom- and problem-oriented, and not performed in a cookbook manner.

17

What Is the Goal of Treating ADD?

I wish ADD were caused by a bug; I would prescribe an antibiotic for seven days and cure it forever. I wish it were caused by a deformity of the brain that I would ask a neurosurgeon to fix. I wish ADD were caused by deficiency of a hormone or a nutrient that I could supply as a medicine; or it could be treated with a pill as headache is by aspirin. I wish a psychologist could treat ADD by talking, peeling off the bad wraps over the scars in the deeper recesses of the mind. Alas, none of the above is true.

ADD is a constitutional disease—a disease whose bearer is born with an imbalance of the chemicals that orchestrate the symphony of the human brain. Discordant notes of this neurochemical symphony result in noisy, disorganized, and unregulated behavior. Unfortunately, the conductor does not know that his production is noisy and disorganized; he cannot do better. It is as if a car has a noisy engine, and the owner can, at best, decrease the noise a little or, at worst, learn to put up with it.

A child is born with ADD. In most cases, it lasts almost a whole lifetime. In the rest, it lasts at least past childhood and into many years of adulthood. The realistic goal of treatment, in the present state of knowledge, is learning to cope and care, not cure (see Figure 6 below). Learning to cope involves understanding the nature of the condition and improving the fit between the child and his or her environment by decreasing environmental demands and distractions. Caring involves helping the child medically, educationally, and socially so that he or she achieves maximally in school, has good relations with parents, siblings, peers, and teachers, becomes a responsible citizen, and, in the words of George Will, the famous political commentator, "learns to give love and take love."

3 C'S OF ADD MANAGEMENT

COPING
Parent education
Teacher education
Guilt-free parenting
Realisitic expectations

CARING
Summer camp
Firm disciplining
Special education
Social skills training
Decreasing environmental distractions
Ongoing teacher-parent communication
Psychotherapy for coexisting disorders
Family therapy for parent-child conflict
Behavior modification for behavior problems

CURING
Medications

Figure 6

"Never, never, never, never, give up."
WINSTON CHURCHILL

18

How Does One Cope with ADD?

Most parents want their children to be flawless, healthy, motivated, and compliant. Any deviation from that ideal causes mental pain. Whereas physical deviations are relatively easier to understand because they are concrete—they can be seen, felt, and touched—behavioral and mental ailments are intriguing because they do not have tangible markers. Society believes that all behavior is driven by external models—good behavior should beget good behavior, and bad behavior is due to bad role models. Parents wonder why their child is behaving abnormally when they have done nothing wrong. It is difficult for them to believe that behavior can be driven by internal forces due to an innate, biologically-based problem. And if they do, it is difficult for them to hold such a child responsible for his or her actions and to apply discipline—as they would any other child—so that he or she learns to live by society's rules despite innate problems. The crux of coping with ADD is striking a balance between these two forces.

Educate yourself about ADD: Parents of children with ADD should educate themselves about the nature and course of this condition so they can make rational choices and informed decisions. They should read books on ADD written by medical and mental health professionals, and attend educational seminars arranged by parent and advocacy groups such as Children with Attention Deficit Disorders (CHADD). If they are still mystified by the bewildering array of myths about the causes and cure of ADD, they should consult a professional to sift the truth from the trash.

Change your attitude about your child's behavior (cognitive restructuring):
There is a general tendency to consider inappropriate behavior of children as
intentional and malevolent. Lewis Carroll poignantly summed up this attitude in
a ditty by the Duchess in *Alice in Wonderland*:

> "Speak roughly to your little boy,
> And beat him when he sneezes:
> He only does it to annoy,
> Because he knows it teases."

Dr. Still, a famous physician at the turn of the past century, called children's
behavioral difficulties problems of moral control. Others have used labels such as
spoiled, poorly brought-up, and undisciplined to describe these children. Instead
of helping them, such epithets deny them the benefit of available treatments and
induce guilt in both parents and children. Parents feel that they did not raise
their children properly. The children think that they are impish and fiendish.
If these children come to believe that they are "bad" or "messed-up", they
internalize a negative narrative of themselves—as did Topsy in *Uncle Tom's
Cabin*—and subsequent treatment becomes difficult:

> "What makes you behave so bad?" said St. Clare. "'Spects it's my
> wicked heart." said Topsy. "I 'spects cause I's so wicked!"

According to a famous psychologist, Arnold J. Sameroff, *cognitive
restructuring* involves a shift in thinking (a reframing of the mind): the
symptoms of ADD are involuntary, due to a disease of the brain, and not
deliberate and premeditated acts of maleficence by the child. The title of the
New York Times bestseller, *Driven to Distraction*, by Edward Hallowell,
succinctly sums up this concept of cognitive restructuring: A child with
ADD does not behave the way he or she does deliberately, but is driven to
behave in that manner by his or her brain. Children with ADD are not
immoral, disobedient, or disrespectful. They are not deliberately trying to
hurt anyone, but they simply cannot help behaving the way they do.
According to Dr. Ross W. Greene—author of *The Explosive Child: A New
Approach for Understanding and Parenting*—easily frustrated, "chronically
inflexible" children would do well if they could. According to him, children
do not do well not because they do not want to, but because they do not

have the skills to do so. Russell Barkley, the famous ADD researcher, believes that most symptoms of ADD occur because these children cannot self-regulate and modulate their behavior.

Restructuring also involves considering possibilities other than "bad behavior" when one encounters unacceptable behavior. For example, if a child does not do what you tell him to do, the child might not have heard you, might not have understood you, might have heard you but was distracted by something more interesting, and, finally, he might have truly forgotten what you asked him to do. Moreover, he may have, in the words of Dr. Greene, difficulty in changing the *cognitive set*—that is, changing the focus of the mind from one activity to another. If a child constantly interrupts you or the teacher, she may have an uncontrollable urge to speak her mind. She may have a rush of ideas that she may be unable to hold back. She may have "ants in her pants" or, more truly descriptive, "ants in her brain."

Does this mean that one should ignore infractions and misconduct of a child with ADD? Certainly not! Parents should set limits and rules that need to be followed at home and at large, but they should not constantly blame the child for his actions. They should not become angry in the process. They should not demean the child, send him through guilt trips, or call him bad, disrespectful, and evil. These accusations can distort the child's personal sense of self-worth and self-identity. The child might consider himself villainous and try to act out this identity, setting the stage for secondary behavior problems.

Cast off the burden of guilt and blame: ADD is not caused by bad parenting. Do not blame yourself or your spouse for your child's ADD. In some families, parents blame each other for their children's behavior, sowing the seeds of marital discord. This process of incrimination is transparently described in a short story, "A Subject of Childhood," by Grace Paley:

> "We got to have a serious talk," he said. "I really can't take these kids...Our bodies should have been all relaxed...No one should've been hurt, Faith."
> "Do you mean it's all my fault you all got hurt?"
> "No doubt about it, Faith, you have done a rotten job."
> "Rotten job?" I said.
> "Lousy," he said.

Children with ADD often behave differently with their mothers and fathers. Therefore, one spouse should believe the other when he or she is relating something about the child. I was once interviewing a mother who brought her son to me for consultation. Her husband also joined, but sat at a distance pouting and refusing to participate. "There is nothing wrong with him. He is just a boy. All boys are a little active. She wants him to become a wimp." The mother turned to him tearfully, "You do not know what I have to go through when you are away. I work hard the whole day to teach him rules and you spoil him in the one hour that you spend with him. You are too lenient."

Grandparents, uncles, and aunts also point fingers at one or both parents for spoiling a child. Teachers blame parents for not being good role models. Occasionally, teachers and others automatically assume that the child has ADD because the mother used drugs and alcohol during pregnancy. Some even attribute a child's ADD to his parents' culture or poverty. According to Judith Rich Harris—author of the book, *The Nurture Assumption: Why Children Turn Out the Way They Do: Parents Matter Less Than You Think and Peers Matter More*—parents have little influence upon how their children develop and behave. "Parenting has been oversold," she says. Child-rearing experts do not agree upon what is good parenting and what is bad. While Dr. Spock declares that any kind of spanking is taboo, Dr. James Dobson—author of *Dare to Discipline* and *The New Dare to Discipline*—prescribes "stinging strokes" in response to defiance.

I think that parents are like the two embankments within which the river of childhood energy flows. The force with which this energy flows is determined by the child and the other forces in the terrain, but the direction in which it flows is shaped by the embankments—the parents. ADD is a disorder of the regulation of this energy due to a dysfunction of the nervous system at the chemical level. Parents, in this scenario, are not responsible for the floods and storms that occur, but can only work to prevent and contain them. Thus, instead of debating about your culpability—burdening yourself with guilt in the process—work to help the child. Do not allow anyone else to blame you for your child's predicament. Guilt will decrease your self-esteem as a parent and may even cause depression. And blame will affect your relations with your spouse and other relatives. With the institution of marriage as it is these days, do not let the ADD of your child be the final straw on the camel's back.

Become desensitized to minor infractions of the child: Do not overcontrol your child; this could kill his or her initiative. Children learn by imitating what others do. If the outcome of imitation is good, they assimilate the imitated action in their repertoire of actions; if not, they do not repeat the action. It is all right for them to make a few mistakes. This is even more true of a child with ADD, because a child with ADD has difficulty in learning from his mistakes. Sometimes, such a child does not even know that he is talking loudly or is being a nuisance. Do not respond to every noise or silly prank of a child with ADD. To stay sane, be thick-skinned and ignore minor infractions. Pick your battles carefully. Remember the saying, "Let the sleeping dogs lie, and the barking dogs bark." However, do not overuse this technique of "planned ignoring," because an attention-seeking child may be forced to seek attention in deviant ways if his parents ignore him completely. It may also decrease his self-esteem, because parents' responses serve as a looking glass through which a child develops his sense of self-worth.

Do not get caught up in a battle of words. If a child with ADD argues, walk away and then return when he is calm. He may not mean what he says. If he uses four-letter words, express your condemnation and disapproval of such words, warn him not to use them, and even give consequences. Although these words are indecent, children often use them mechanically without a sexual connotation. We are not living in the age of Victorian respectability, but in the age of Holden Caulfield of *Catcher in the Rye*. Today's adolescents do not believe in "goddamn, David Copperfield kind of crap" as J.D. Salinger's protagonist, Holden, says. They say "puke," "piss," and "shit," but no one really pisses when he says that he is "pissed off," and no one really actually does when he says that he "gives a shit." They do not mean these words, and may not even know their meaning. They use them anyway to sound cool and rebellious to their peers. This is more common for a child with ADD who has low self-esteem, but wants to be accepted in a group.

Every generation has its own slang. Parents should not judge the propriety of language by the standards of their generation, because the colloquialisms used by children today may have lost the vulgar connotations of the past. Parents should avoid angry responses to such words, and certainly not return the fire using similar words.

Children sometimes displace their anger at others onto their parents. Parents are safe outlets for venting frustrations with the whole world. Parents should not take everything a child says to them literally, but should scratch the surface to look beyond the words.

Join a support group of parents of children with ADD: There are many national organizations serving individuals with ADD, with local chapters throughout the United States. The addresses and phone numbers of three such organizations are given below:

Children and Adults with Attention Deficit Disorder (CHADD)
8181 Professional Plaza
Suite 201
Landover, Maryland 20785
Phone: (800) 233-4050
Web site: www.chadd.org

National Attention Deficit Disorder Association (NADDA)
1788 Second Street
Suite 200
Highland Park, Illinois 60035
Phone: (847) 432-ADDA (2332)
Web site: www.add.org

Learning Disabilities Association of America (LDA)
4156 Library Road
Pittsburgh, Pennsylvania 15234-1349
Phone: (412) 341-1515
Web site: www.ldanatl.org

Help your child to cope with ADD: Be an "emotion coach" for your child. Be sensitive to your child's feelings, even if his feelings are intense and out-of-sync with the mood of the moment. If a child is yelling profanely at a sibling who took his teddy bear without asking him, say, "You appear angry. What's the matter?" If the child responds, "He took my teddy bear," validate the child's feelings by saying, "That's not right. I understand why you're angry. Let's think what we can do." Do not yell back at the child, "Don't you curse at your brother. I'll send you to your room next time you do that."

Help children—those with ADD, their siblings and friends—to look beyond the surface to understand their own behavior and that of others. Teach them to ascribe others' actions correctly—to understand that things are not always done to them, but sometimes just happen. A younger brother who is bothered by a class bully may become so caught up in imagining a fight with that classmate, that he punches his older brother, who just happens to be nearby. A classmate of a child with ADD might have bumped shoulders at lunchtime by mistake, not on purpose to show contempt or cause trouble.

Teach children to solve their problems by generating alternatives for them, by walking them through the process. "It is OK to feel angry sometimes, but it is not OK to get mad. Tell your brother that you're angry because he took your teddy bear without asking you. Tell him that it is not right to take things that belong to others without permission, and that you are going to tell Mommy and Daddy."

Learning to become an emotion coach requires parents to examine and shape their own behavior before they begin to coach their child. At the end of the day, parents should analyze their behavior. Did they have any unpleasant exchanges with each other, their children, or others? How did they act in these situations? Why did others behave the way they did? Did they respond to others appropriately or not? This exercise will help them in understanding the behavior of others and to refine their own responses. Spouses can help each other in this process by analyzing and critiquing each other's behavior. For example, a harried husband comes home after driving for two hours in prime-time traffic, and, as soon as he enters the house, his wife asks him if he brought milk from the supermarket or not. He flips out and answers, "What do you think: I'm a milkman?!" His wife retorts, "Don't you yell at me. I'm not a maid either." And the battle of words escalates, spoiling the evening. On quiet reflection after their anger burns out, the wife realizes that she should have waited for a few minutes before demanding the carton of milk, realizing that her husband might have been delayed in a traffic jam; and the husband apologizes for having reacted so negatively, knowing that his wife was not aware that the traffic was bad. Such kind of introspection teaches one to look beyond surface behavior and makes behavioral responses reflective as opposed to impulsive.

Help the child understand himself: Children fantasize about their problems, often in a manner that provokes anxiety and worry. It is, therefore, important to explain to children with ADD that their attentional difficulties and hyperactivity are due to a disease called ADD. Informing children about their condition (technically called "disclosure") is a double-edged sword. It can have a positive effect, such as improving compliance with medications, or it can become an excuse for them to behave abnormally. It can relieve their confusion about their own behavior, or it can depress them by confirming that they are, indeed, different from others. Nevertheless, the self-concept of being different is more acceptable than the self-concept of being bad.

How to inform a child depends upon a child's age and ability to understand. It is futile to attempt to inform a preschool children that they have ADD, because they do not have the intelligence or insight to understand the concept. One should, on the other hand, always try to inform school-age children that they have ADD. There is no universally accepted technique of informing young school-age children that they have ADD. I use the following analogies and examples:

• A car driver should focus on the road and control the steering wheel while driving. You are not able to focus on the road. Your steering control is not good. Therefore, you go off the road and bump into other cars. You are unable to apply the brakes when you should. Some cars have strong brakes and some have loose brakes. You, like a car with loose brakes, are unable to stop when you apply the brakes.

• As suggested by Dr. Melvin Levine—director of The Clinical Center for the Study of Development and Learning, University of North Carolina—one can give explanations by using an analogy of a cockpit with control panels to children who like planes. The pilot can fly the plane only if he is able to focus on the panels, control his speed and direction, and apply the brakes when needed.

• The life of a child with ADD is like a classroom without a teacher or a grocery store without a manager. I tell children that a certain part of our brain works as a teacher who directs us in what to do, telling us to pay attention when we are distracted and to stay still when we are fidgety or hyper. In some children this teacher is tough—like Mr. Feeny of the popular television sitcom *Boy Meets World*—and in some he is lenient—like Jonathan in the same show. In the former case, the children stay in their seats and pay attention and, in the latter, they talk unnecessarily and move around the classroom.

• For children fond of television, I use examples from their favorite television shows. Most children know Steve Urkel of *Family Matters* and Kimmy Gibbler of *Full House*. Steve is clumsy, talks too much, interrupts others, and cannot stay still. Kimmy is socially inept and intrusive. Both can be used to help a child with ADD understand his behaviors. Steve Urkel is a particularly good example for explaining that ADD is not due to poor intelligence, but due to lack of control. For younger children, cartoon characters from television and movies can be used to explain their behavior. Angelica in *Rug Rats* serves as a good analogy for an aggressive toddler. She is mean and bullies younger rug rats.

Children are especially receptive to learning about themselves in moments of distress. If your child is upset because children in his school call him hyper or crazy, do not shut him up by saying, "Don't worry." Validate his feelings. Say, "Honey, I know how it feels. I know you do not mean to disturb others. It happens because you cannot control yourself." Use one of the explanations suggested above. Try to explain to your child what the epithets used by other children mean. Teach your child either to ignore such attacks or plan ways with him to counter them. Teach him how to control his anger and to channel his frustrations positively. Support the child as he attempts to understand himself and tries to adapt his behaviors accordingly. Emphasize that he is different, not deviant. Emphasize that he has a disorder, but is not helpless. He can overcome his problems with effort.

"Discipline but not restraint is the technique, discipline leading to self-management, and joy should be part of that discipline."

PEARL S. BUCK, *The Joy of Children*

19

How Does One Care for a Child with ADD?

Caring for a child with ADD involves making lifestyle adjustments to improve the goodness of fit between the parents and the child and between the school and the child. It also involves imparting those skills to the child that would help him or her in adapting to his or her environment.

ENVIRONMENTAL ADJUSTMENTS AT HOME

Minimize distractions: Provide a quiet, distraction-free environment for homework. Pull down the drapes, switch off the television, and turn off the telephone ringer. If you can afford to, soundproof the walls and ceiling of the child's room, or buy a cubicle-type workstation. Use a table lamp instead of diffuse light. Turn off all the televisions in the house when the child does his homework, because children with ADD may be distracted even by noise from other rooms. A radio, on the other hand, may be left on, depending on the child's preference. A few children work better with background music, which competes with noise, preventing it from getting the mind's attention. In one research study, children were found to solve arithmetic problems better when they listened to their favorite music.

Structure the environment of your child: Act as a personal valet for your child, because a child with ADD lacks the capacity to plan and organize his environment. Structure his environment and organize his days and nights.

Set a consistent daily routine: For example, wake the child at a fixed time, say 7:30 A.M. (set an alarm); give her breakfast at 8:30 A.M. and an after-school snack at 3:30 P.M.; take her to the park from 4:00 to 4:30 P.M.; have her do homework from 5:00 P.M. to 6:00 P.M.; serve dinner from 6:00 to 6:30 P.M.; allow television from 6:30 to 8:00 P.M.; spend some quality time with her from 8:00 to 8:30 P.M.; and put her to bed at 9:00 P.M. Use concrete reminders—such as Post-it notes and refrigerator notices—to remind her of her schedule.

Organize his closet at home: Put his clothes neatly in easy-to-find places. Organize his desk at home. Keep his books and notebooks in order. Put up a bulletin board on his wall. Organize his book bag so that he can find his notebooks and pencils easily.

Children with ADD often have perceptual problems, that is, they may not see things around them as others do. Therefore, do not be upset if posters in your child's room do not appear straight or if he is unable to set the dinner table properly. Either ignore it or assist him in putting things straight, without undue criticism.

Prepare and plan for transitions in advance: Children with ADD have difficulty in changing their mindset quickly from sleep to wakefulness, from play to work, and from work to sleep. Give these children extra time to wake up and get ready for school. Bear with them if they continue to play when they are supposed to start homework. Be patient with them if they take a long time to go to sleep at night. They also have difficulty adapting to new places and people.

Going to a new school or to a new house is difficult for any child, but for a child with ADD it may be overwhelming. She may fuss, whine, and act out. Do not react if she acts out. Prepare yourself and your child for transitions. Inform your child well in advance if you are planning to move to another apartment or are planning to change her school. Take time off from work to oversee important transitions. Prepare teachers in advance. For example, inform the kindergarten teacher that your child may cry longer than other children of her age. Support your child in coping with the stress of transition. Let her maintain continuity as much as possible— for example, arrange the furniture in the same way as it was in the previous apartment and display pictures of her old friends on her bedroom wall. Allow her to make frequent phone calls to her old friends for a few days. Praise her coping efforts, however tumultuous the transition 1s.

Periodically refocus the child to the relevant task: Use cues and prompts—such as signs, flash cards, "traffic signals," and alarm clocks—to remind and refocus the child. Nonverbal prompts and cues are better than verbal refocusing, because they are not accompanied by emotional overtones of words.

Avoid overstimulation: Do not allow children to watch noisy, violent, and overstimulating television programs, such as *Mighty Morphin Power Rangers* and *Child's Play*. Review television programs that your child watches and block those that are labeled as violent or vulgar. Buy a television with a V-chip so that you can enforce rules; merely asking a child not to watch bad programs usually does not work. Limit the use of boom boxes. Dim the lights and turn off the television at bedtime.

ENVIRONMENTAL ADJUSTMENTS AT SCHOOL

Seating: Seat an inattentive child in the front so that she is not disturbed by other children in the classroom and the teacher is able to redirect her unobtrusively. A hyperactive child, on the other hand, should be seated in the back row to allow him to stretch or walk in the aisle without disturbing other children.

If a child cannot function in the mainstream, a smaller self-contained class with a high teacher-student ratio may be necessary. In such cases, the child will have to be classified as emotionally disturbed to qualify for special education.

Curriculum modifications: The teacher should break down information into smaller units, use simple language, and repeat information without becoming aggravated. Abstract concepts should be taught as concretely as possible, even if one has to use analogies, parables, or personification. Multisensory technique—such as teaching counting with an abacus—using the senses of touch, sight, and sound should be used to capture and sustain attention. *Sesame Street* uses this technique very effectively. The teacher should explore what sensory modality captures the child's attention. If a child is more responsive to visual material, the teacher should modify the instructional strategy to present teaching material visually. If your child frequently forgets his homework, ask his teacher to write down the child's homework assignments on a memo pad. See the memo pad daily and initial it when he completes his work.

IMPROVE COMMUNICATION

State expectations clearly, in simple sentences, and in the "I" format: "Honey, I want you to do your homework now," instead of "Do your homework now."

Be concrete: For example, instead of saying, "I would like you to finish tables before you do word problems," say, "I would like you to finish questions 1 to 6 before you attempt questions 7 to 12." Break down complex and long instructions into simple steps, giving one instruction at a time.

Be specific: Instead of saying, "I want your room to be cleaned by the time I get out of the shower," say, "Put your clothes in the hamper, change the bed sheets, change your pillow covers, and vacuum your room while I am in the shower."

Provide immediate feedback: If you have asked your child to clean his room and have been specific about what you mean by that, and the room is not cleaned as advised, immediately tell the child again what was needed and wanted.

Repeat, repeat, and repeat: Children with ADD process information slowly and superficially. Statements such as, "She has a thick head," "It goes in one ear and out the other," and "Nothing sinks in that head" may literally be true for a child with ADD. Therefore, do not be offended if the child has to be repeatedly told or shown to do something.

Be a patient listener: Try to figure out why the child is saying what he is saying by listening carefully. A few children with ADD talk unnecessarily, yapping all the time. If your child is hyper-tongued, you may have to learn to ignore him. Do not interrupt or cut a child off even if she is talking slowly. Learn to refocus conversation if it goes off on a tangent.

Do not overreact to the onslaught of words: If you get involved in a battle of words, the real issue may never be known. For example, if a child says, "I hate you," she may not mean it. Children often displace anger at others onto their parents.

Maintain eye contact while talking to your children: Show that you are interested by your facial response and by supporting words like, "I know how you feel."

If there is complete breakdown of civil communication in the family, with members shouting or yelling at each other, or passing sarcastic remarks, or not talking to each other, seek professional help from a family therapist.

TEACH THE CHILD SELF-CONTROL

The ability of a child to exercise self-control depends on his developmental level. A toddler is unlikely to be aware that he is hyperactive and may not be able to control himself, even when asked by his parents to do so. He may have to be physically held and taken to a less stimulating environment. An early-grade school child should be able to control himself when asked by his parents to stop. His parents can either ask him or show him a card with "Stop, listen, and think" written on it, whenever he is fidgety. An older child, on the other hand, can be taught to identify signs of hyperactivity and to control herself whenever she notices herself out of control. She can carry the "Stop, listen, and think" card in her pocket to remind her whenever she feels distracted and/or hyper. Or the child can carry a tape recorder programmed to ask every thirty minutes, "Was I paying attention?" He can record his responses in a notebook and, based upon these, he can grade his own behavior at the end of the day.

Help the child to understand his and others' feelings and his responses to these feelings. Teach him about facial expressions of happiness, sadness, anger, and surprise by showing cartoons or line drawings. If the child appears mad, make a statement, such as "You seem mad," or if he is very happy at something, "You look very excited."

If your child is angry, ask him to go to his room and cool off. Do not try to reason with your child when he is angry. Children are unreceptive to suggestions when they are angry. They may become even more aggravated and make negative statements, such as "Are you a mind reader?" or "Leave me alone." After the crisis is over, sit down with your child, recreate the scenario, and help him to learn where he went wrong. Help him to generate alternative solutions by role-playing.

Create additional vignettes to drive home the point. For example, if your child pushes and hurts his younger sister when she tries to play with his Nintendo, empathize with him—"it was not right for her to play with his Nintendo without your permission"—but tell him assertively that pushing the younger child was not the right thing to do. Ask the older child if he could have reacted differently. Help him generate alternatives to pushing, such as firmly telling his sister not to touch the Nintendo because it does not belong to her, or telling Mom or Dad that she was bothering him.

Teach the child to make self-statements, such as "I am getting mad, I can handle it, I need to chill out," if she feels that she is getting angry. Subvocalization is an important method by which children direct themselves. Failure of this skill is one of the key problems in ADD, according to ADD researcher Russell Barkley. Lewis Carroll's legendary character Alice used this technique to survive in her Wonderland: "'Come, there is no use in crying like that!' said Alice to herself rather sharply. 'I advise you to leave off this minute!' She generously gave herself very good advice."

Teach the child to learn the physical accompaniments of emotion. Each emotion is accompanied by a certain response of the body. For example, an angry person's heart beats faster, her face becomes contorted, and her muscles become tense. Happiness has exactly the opposite response: decreased heart rate and muscle relaxation. If a child learns to control the bodily responses to emotion, control of the feeling component follows as a corollary. Based on this premise, a child can be taught to control her body in order for her to control her mind. Ask the child to walk slowly, like a penguin. Teach the child to gradually stretch her body like a robot and then to relax it like a rag doll to feel the tension of her muscles. Teach her simple yoga postures, such as a) stretching vertically with hands upwards; b) bending down at the waist to touch the toes; c) bending sideways; d) touching the toes with one hand, the other hand raised upwards in the opposite direction; and e) stretching the back backwards. Stretching the various parts of the body slowly through yoga gives a sense of mastery to the child, a feeling that she can control her movements voluntarily. Teaching her to concentrate on the flame of a candle is a good technique for learning to stay focused.

Two other methods can be taught to increase a child's attention span.

• Ask the child to read a book without getting up or talking for five minutes, to earn a star. Gradually increase the time to ten and fifteen minutes. "Cash" five to seven stars for a reward.

• Institute "neutral time," that is, time in which phones are off the hook, no television or radio is on, and everyone in the family is reading or contemplating, to recharge their batteries, as it were.

It is important that parents practice what they preach and be good role models for their children. Parents should avoid impulsive responses to their children and spouses. For example, a child comes home from school and his father asks him, "How was school?" The child angrily replies, "What's it to you?" The father yells back, "Don't you talk to me like that," and the horns get locked. The parent should think of alternatives for why the child behaved that way. "Did someone bother you at school? You look upset. What is the matter?" Once the child is in a good mood, talk to him about his behavior, and explain to him what was wrong. Parents should tell real or fictional vignettes of arguments and scuffles to their children and discuss with them why people behaved in a particular manner in those situations—and how they should have behaved. Television shows and movies can serve as important focal points of discussion.

Do not post aphorisms such as "Haste makes waste," "Think before you speak," or "Look before you leap," on the refrigerator or bathroom walls, because children do not care for these hackneyed phrases. Older children and adolescents respond, "Yeah-yeah-yeah," and the younger ones do not understand them.

Ideally, a schoolteacher should also participate in teaching a child self-monitoring and self-regulation by role-playing, by showing the child on-task and off-task behaviors, and by teaching the child to monitor the quality of his effort.

Encourage children to solve their own problems, even if they make mistakes. If the child makes an honest mistake, tell him it is OK to make a mistake and that we can all make mistakes. No one is perfect. The ability to solve their own problems gives children a sense of mastery.

If your child is resistant to your suggestions and help, seek professional help. Formal therapy to improve self-monitoring and self-regulating skills is called *cognitive-behavioral therapy* (*CBT*). The paradigm underlying CBT is that cognition (thoughts, such as plans, goals, beliefs, and self-statements) strongly influences the mood and the behavior of a child. According to Lauren Braswell and Michael Bloomquist, pioneers of CBT, this therapy increases a child's ability to think about what he is supposed to do in a particular situation by teaching him the connection between means and ends (planning to achieve a goal), actions and consequences (ability to think about the consequences of actions), and causal thinking (ability to think why something happened). It also teaches a child to solve problems by generating alternative solutions. In short, it teaches the child to think before he acts. CBT is provided either individually or in groups to children over eight years of age.

Besides teaching self-regulation, an important goal of CBT is to correct wrong ways of thinking, called *cognitive distortions*. Children with ADD often blame others for their mistakes: "I hit him because he was bothering me." They do not accept responsibility for their behavior: "I didn't do anything wrong, but the teacher was mean to me." Correcting cognitive distortions requires professional help, because children with ADD perceive the world differently than we do.

SOCIAL-SKILLS TRAINING

Social-skills training is provided by social workers, school counselors, and psychologists through verbal and written instructions, role-playing, and feedback. The aims of social-skills training are:

• **to improve pro-social behavior, such as sharing and taking turns:** Taking turns can be taught by playing a game in which a teddy bear or ball is passed around in a circle of children, and only the person with the bear or the ball can speak.

• **to increase capacity for intimacy, concern, and gratitude:** Once again, this is done by serving as good role models. If parents do not thank anyone and are not civil or polite, their children are not going to be polite. Take the child to a homeless shelter or a soup kitchen on Thanksgiving, and encourage him to collect money or things for a good cause, such as hurricane relief.

• **to improve feelings of empathy:** To have empathy is to feel as others feel and to look at things from another's point of view. Empathy can be taught by role-playing and by discussing television shows or real-life incidents.

• **to help control anger:** Teach the child to identify and control his feelings of anger in order to avoid trouble and to diffuse tension. Teach the following techniques for avoiding trouble caused by anger:

> **Ignoring:** Avoid trouble by avoiding the provoker and ignoring her remarks when she dares you, just as you walk away from a barking dog.
> **Anticipation and self-statements:** Prepare for unpleasant

situations in advance. For example, if a bully is advancing, start making quiet, self-statements such as, "He is coming, but I don't want to get in trouble. I will stay cool. I will take deep breaths."

Humor: George Bernard Shaw and someone else were jostling to get into an opera house in Paris when the latter angrily pushed Shaw back, saying, "I do not let ruffians go before me." Shaw turned this angry altercation into a humorous one by stepping aside, saying, "I always let ruffians pass by."

Stress ball: Squeeze a spongy ball hidden in your pocket as hard as you can.

Deep breaths: Close your eyes and slowly breathe through your nose, taking in as much air as you can. Then exhale slowly, letting out as much air as you can. Repeat this cycle five times.

Counting backwards: Start loudly with 20 and count backwards— 19, 18, 17, and on—diffusing tension in the process of counting backwards.

Imagining: Counteract the feelings of anger and stress by imagining some past pleasurable experience.

If some tension still lingers, the child should try to relax by sitting in a comfortable chair in a comfortable position without crossing her legs, with her hands at her side, eyes closed, and first tighten her muscles like a robot and then relax them like a rag doll.

Many programs for teaching emotional skills to young children are being researched in the United States at present. In a project backed by the National Institute of Mental Health, at Chapel Hill, North Carolina, children are learning to develop empathy, anger control, and anger control, through a twenty-eight-lesson Seattle program, called the *Second Step*.

DISCIPLINING A CHILD WITH ADD (CIVILIZING HUCK)

Discipline consists of teaching a child to recognize and act within acceptable norms of behavior. Its goal should be to change future behavior rather than to punish past behavior. Given below are a few guidelines for parents:

- Discipline by a judicious mixture of love and reprimand, with the aim of teaching the child to develop self-control. Through discipline, children internalize the values of the family and become responsible for their own behavior.

- Do not feel guilty when you discipline a child. "I do not want to hurt him. He is so tiny," a mother said tearfully to me, while her son went on a rampage in my office. You are not hurting your child by disciplining him. In fact, you are insulating him against future injuries by teaching him self-control. Discipline is a basic need of a child, as are love and security.

- The method of discipline should be consistent with the age and developmental level of the child. Preaching and pleading with a toddler is as ineffective as a time-out is with an adolescent.

- Know what you are correcting (behavioral analysis). Identify problem behaviors by keeping a log of good behaviors, minor infractions, and unacceptable behaviors of the child for one or two weeks. From the list of unacceptable behaviors, identify one or two of the most unacceptable behaviors as target behaviors for modification. Write the setting, antecedents, description of behavior, and consequences (abc's) of such behaviors.

- Reward good behaviors (positive reinforcement). *Positive reinforcement* for good behavior should be immediate for toddlers and delayed for older kids. A hug, an encouraging remark, a kiss, a lollipop, or anything a child likes can be a reward. While a toddler should get his reward right after the behavior, an older child should earn a star or token for each good behavior or each good day. A certain number of tokens or stars should earn him a reward at the end of the week. Do not give too many rewards. Keep the ratio of compliments to reprimands no more than three to one; otherwise the child will become addicted to praise and rewards.

- Punish unacceptable behaviors by giving unpleasant consequences (*negative reinforcement*). If any rule is broken, agreed-upon consequences should follow immediately. Once the child has borne the consequence of his action, everyone should go on with their lives as usual. Parents should not nag the child. Empty threats and nagging do not work and only worsen the behavior. Similarly, verbal and physical reprimands generate anger and usually do not have a lasting effect. However, a swat on the hands or the backside is not child abuse. I agree with Lawrence Diller, author of *Running on Ritalin*, that children with ADD—the so-called difficult or strong-willed children—require an authoritative and, sometimes, an authoritarian method of discipline—one that administers a negative consequence to the child immediately, even if it involves physically restraining and punishing the child. The following techniques may be used for negative reinforcement of unacceptable behaviors:

   Time-out: A child sits in a boring place—such as in a corner of a room, or facing the wall, or in the bathroom—for a preset amount of time as a consequence of bad behavior. A time-out is calculated as one minute per year of age. For example, a five-year-old child who breaks a house rule should sit in an unstimulating area of the house for five minutes. A time-out should be monitored with a kitchen timer; the timer should be reset if the child gets up from the time-out spot before the buzzer goes off. Enforcing time-out in a child with ADD is a daunting task in the beginning, because the child tests the parents by getting up again and again from his seat. Patiently and firmly take him back to the seat each time he gets up, until he learns that Mom means business. Do not give in to the child's sweet talk, but firmly state that he will have to sit in time-out for what he did, but he will not have time-out in the future if he does not misbehave. Do not get angry. Time-out is effective from three-to-five years of age until about ten or eleven years.

   Loss of privileges—such as television—if the child fails to follow rules: Do not melt when you hear, "I'm sorry, Mom," but tell the child that she has to pay the price now, although she can appeal later. Never give an empty threat. If you tell the child to finish her homework before she can watch television, do not let her watch television, even if it means pulling the plug.

   Response cost: If the child breaks a rule, depending on how serious the offense is, deduct a percentage from his allowance for that week. If a child receives ten dollars as a weekly allowance and fails to finish his homework, he loses two dollars of it. An older child who earns some money should actually pay from his earnings if he damages property.

Contingency contracting: If a teenager repeatedly breaks house rules—such as night curfew—write up a contract with her that she will have to move out if she comes home late again.

Over-correction: Ask the child to correct the adverse effects of inappropriate behavior and to practice appropriate behavior. For example, the penalty for dawdling or making a mess at the dinner table might be cleaning up the mess and doing the dishes.

Systematic ignoring: If your youngster tries to seek your attention negatively by pulling a prank, act as if you did not see anything.

- Be consistent. Children are great masqueraders. When they are caught on the wrong foot, they will do anything to escape the punishment. They will argue, lie, negotiate, plead, even kiss-up with folded hands. They will promise, "Please give me one more chance. I won't do it again." They may even play one parent against the other. Do not give in. Stay firm as would a parking-violations ticket officer. Tell the child, "Pay now and plead later." Inconsistency is the worst enemy of discipline and a sure way of spoiling your children.

- Although you should enforce the house rules consistently and firmly, do not convert your house into West Point. Try to resolve minor conflicts by negotiations. If a teenager insists on going to a party that you do not approve of, negotiate a deal, such as a curfew and no alcohol. Offer a few acceptable behaviors in lieu of the unacceptable behavior. The ability to make a choice saves face for the youngster and avoids power struggles.

- All the adults in the family should agree on what behaviors are unacceptable and on the consequences of such behavior. The children should be invited to participate in making these ground rules, but parents should take the lead and should be in command. According to Stanley Turecki, the author of *Difficult Child,* too much democracy in the family is bad. Once the rules have been agreed upon, everyone in the family should abide by them.

Teenagers—tough nuts to crack: Both body and mind undergo tremendous changes during adolescence. The body becomes too tall or remains too small, the face becomes too hairy in girls or remains hairless in boys, and the breasts become too big or remain too small. These bodily changes cause stress. In addition, the mind grapples with the issue of separating from the parents to become independent (psychologically called *separation and individuation*). With few avenues to vent their feelings, fears, and fantasies without being judged, teenagers either withdraw or act out.

Friends are the most important allies of teenagers in the process of adjusting to these changes. They are going through similar changes, they can confide in one another, and they provide security that hitherto their parents were providing. Therefore, teenagers hang together, a process called *peer bonding*. It is healthy and not a sign of rebellion or love lost. Although parents should watch what kind of company a child keeps, there is often little that they can do to influence the process. Usually birds of a feather flock together. Studious types find studious friends, and athletic types find other sportsmen. Friends are sacrosanct; a teenager should never be shamed in front of them, nor should the friends be slighted or judged. Teenagers would do anything to be accepted in their peer group. Often smoking, wilding, and other such behaviors start in this manner.

In addition to bodily changes, a teenager's mind grapples with the issues of separating from parents to become independent (psychologically called *separation and individuation*). One of the unfortunate consequences of this emotional separation is teenagers' mistrust of adults. Teenagers view adults with the attitude "us against them" and, in extreme cases, may even fantasize stories of pressure and abuse by their parents. Like Alice in Wonderland, their perceptions are distorted and their feelings are out of sync with reality. This phenomenon should not be taken personally by parents. They misinterpret their parents' intentions, even if good, and ignore their friends' conduct, even if harmful.

Teenagers with ADD have these feelings multiplied many times over because of their difficulty with transitions and their apprehension about going into the real world, being aware that they are different from others. They may either isolate themselves socially or make delinquent friends. Socially isolated children are at a high risk of making abnormal liaisons in cyberspace. Children with ADD are more likely to put themselves in harm's way by acting impulsively to be accepted by their peer group. They may refuse to take prescribed medications or to participate in counseling because they do not want to singled out as abnormal. Teenagers with ADD are also at high risk for substance abuse.

These are difficult times for both children and their parents. Both require additional help and support. Parents should avoid knee-jerk responses, should not take negative pronouncements of hate and rejection personally, but should be watchful—in both the real and the cyber world—without being intrusive, and should be available for emotional support when sought.

PSYCHOTHERAPY

Simply stated, psychotherapy is the process of treating the mind by changing the manner in which it thinks, feels, and looks at the world (perceives reality). Psychotherapy assists the patient in changing reality or in accepting reality if it cannot be changed. Psychotherapy can be supportive, psychodynamic, or psychoanalytic. In supportive psychotherapy, the therapist assists the child in coping with the real world, failure, rejection, anger, and the feeling of being different or damaged due to ADD. He or she provides a forum where the child can vent his or her feelings, without the fear of retribution or judgment. The therapist assists the child in looking at and understanding the world rationally, and in understanding relationships. He or she builds the child's self-esteem by pointing out the child's strengths. He or she teaches the child how to solve problems and to resolve day to day conflicts of discipline, relationships, and school work. A supportive psychotherapist helps the family to cope, as well, through information and education.

In psychodynamic psychotherapy, the therapist analyzes the manner in which the mind thinks or feels and why it feels that way, and helps the child to gain more insight into his or her own problems and to modify his or her own behavior. Psychodynamic psychotherapy looks at the external world—the child's family, parents, siblings, and peers—as the source of conflict. Although it delves into the mind and its past, it does not try to unearth the subconscious. The focus is on the present and future and not on the remote past.

Psychoanalytic psychotherapy, on the other hand, attempts to access and address internal conflicts, often originating in the earliest experiences of the child. Whereas the aim of psychodynamic psychotherapy is to increase the patient's understanding of the world and his responses to it, the aim of psychoanalytic psychotherapy is to expose and resolve suppressed conflicts so that they no longer exert internal pressure on the individual. According to this school of therapy, children behave abnormally because of subconscious emotional scars they sustained while negotiating some of the emotional milestones of earlier development. For example, a child who had trouble separating from his mother at the age of three years may later have trouble going off to kindergarten, may have difficulty socializing with the other children and dating, and may well have trouble leaving home when the time comes. Psychoanalysis creates a situation in which the child's past conflicts (problems) come alive in the treatment room and can be dealt with in "real time," worked out with a sympathetic, nonjudgmental professional whose job is to help youngsters understand themselves better. The child/adolescent psychoanalyst works with the younger child through play, and with the older child and adolescent through talking. Psychoanalytic psychotherapy is very costly and is rarely used nowadays.

Individual psychotherapy is required if a child has severe emotional problems and conduct disorders. Family therapy may be required if there is marital discord, adult-child and child-child conflicts, and total breakdown of communication among family members.

Whereas supportive psychotherapy can be given by a social worker or a psychologist, psychodynamic and psychoanalytic psychotherapy should be given either by a psychologist or a psychiatrist. Usually psychotherapy is given weekly in forty-five-minute to one-hour sessions.

Sometimes supportive therapy is provided by one therapist to a group of six to eight children. The therapist works on impulse or anger control, and teaches children social skills. Other goals in such groups are teaching nonviolent methods of conflict resolution, how to communicate with peers, and how to make friends. Knowing that there are other children who have problems similar to theirs may be therapeutic for some children.

Contrary to popular belief, psychotherapy and counseling alone cannot cure ADD, because ADD is not caused by emotional conflicts, but by a chemical imbalance in the brain. Russell Barkley, a famous ADD researcher, divided 200 children between the ages of four-and-a-half and six years, with IQs above 80, into a counseling and a no counseling group. One hundred and sixty children, and their parents, in the counseling group received therapy; and the parents also received training in how to deal with their children. The forty age-matched children in the no-counseling group only attended regular kindergarten classes at the researcher's facility. After four years, the researchers did not find a significant difference between the two groups. A review article that appeared in a 1994 issue of *Archives of Family Medicine* concluded that methylphenidate improves behavior and academic performance, while cognitive-behavioral and family therapies, although intuitively appealing, have a rather weak effect.

The National Institute of Mental Health sponsored a multicenter study that compared drug and nondrug approaches to the treatment of ADD. After a fourteen-month trial, the researchers concluded that "medication management alone or in combination with intensive behavioral treatments was better than behavioral treatments alone" in uncomplicated ADD, whereas combined medication and behavioral treatments were better than the routine care offered by community pediatricians—mostly medications—for symptoms such as aggression, oppositional-defiant behavior, and poor social functioning. Intensive psychosocial therapy and nondrug approaches did not offer any measurable benefit to children with uncomplicated ADD, whereas medications were found to be superior to psychosocial treatments for ADD symptoms. The study included 579 children between the ages of seven and nine years at the following medical centers across the United States and Canada: New York State Psychiatric Institute, Duke University, University of California—at Berkeley and Irvine—University of Pittsburgh, and McGill University, Montreal, Canada.

The psychosocial interventions in this study were very intense, including thirty training sessions for parents, a summer camp to improve the child's social and learning skills, daily behavior report cards, eight weeks of teacher training sessions, and an in-school paraprofessional who helped the child to stay focused in the classroom. Such intense intervention is not likely to be available for most children for fiscal and other reasons. Parents may not have time for 30 training sessions because both of them work; summer camps are very costly; teachers may not have time to write and review daily behavior report cards when they have twenty-five to thirty children in the classroom; and an individual paraprofessional for every child with ADD certainly would send the board of education budget through the roof.

BUILDING THE CHILD'S SELF-ESTEEM

An important goal of caring for children with ADD is to build their sense of self-worth—their feeling OK about themselves despite their problems. The self-narrative we want a child with ADD to have is: "I am different, but I am loved by my parents the way I am. At least I am trying. I may not be able to stay still, but I get my work done. I may not be good at baseball, but I am good at chores." We do not want the child to think: "I am screwed up, I am messed up. Nothing is going to make any difference. They do not like me the way I am, because they keep trying to fix me all the time." Social-skills training involves teaching children to look at their strengths, not to be overly critical of themselves and others, and not to misconstrue others' statements. Social-skills training involves training parents as well, because parents are the mirrors at which the children look for self-reaffirmation. If parents communicate by their statements, body language, and attitude to their child that he is not OK, no amount of "I love you, honey" is going to work. Parents should identify and glorify the strengths of children and the small steps they make, instead of obsessing about their weaknesses. All children are different, and everyone has a few weaknesses. Big deal. Everyone has a role to play in this world. Parents should examine their own feelings of inadequacy. Are they trying to fix themselves through their child? Instead of trying to "fix" and correct the child all the time, they should spend one-half to one hour daily with the child doing activities that do not involve correction and direction.

In today's culture, "average children" are not valued. The school system spends an inordinate amount of money and effort at the extreme ends of the bell-shaped curve of intelligence: with extremely intelligent children, to get them on honor rolls; and with profoundly retarded children, to reaffirm their own humanity. Potential Ivy Leaguers become sacred cows secluded in honors classes. The athletically-smart obtain a celebrity status. Average children just drift by, struggling to be acknowledged and recognized. A child with ADD is more likely than not to be in this category. Parents and schools should help these youngsters to feel that they are loved and accepted as much as anyone else.

20

Is There an Antibiotic for ADD?

Since time immemorial Man has been searching for a panacea—a drug—that will cure all maladies, physical and mental. Although the goal of a cure-all is as remote today as it was in antiquity, with the discovery of antibiotics and genetically and chemically engineered drugs in the twentieth century, the goal of a specific drug for each disease appears within reach. We do not have a magic pill for ADD yet, but, theoretically, it is a distinct possibility because ADD is, most likely, caused by a chemical imbalance. Indeed, about three-quarters of the children who are treated with medications for ADD benefit from them, whereas the majority of the children who are treated without medications—with the various therapies described in the previous chapter—continue to have significant problems. Drugs decrease impulsivity and motor restlessness and improve social behavior and attention, indirectly improving academic performance. Better academic performance, in turn, improves self-esteem and social acceptance. Parent/child and teacher/child conflicts ameliorate as the child becomes more responsive to parents' and teachers' requests.

Although some religious groups and naturopaths take a strong exception to the "desecration of the body" by extraneous chemicals—especially those for a disease of the mind—taking an additional chemical is like adding a drop in the ocean of chemicals that make up the body. The human body is a soup of tens of thousands of chemicals, such as hormones, enzymes, and neurotransmitters. Almost every process in the body—from digesting the food that we eat to unfolding the genetic information that we inherit from our parents—is chemical. Each organ of the body is like a sea in this vast ocean, each with its own array of chemicals. Of the myriad chemicals that make up the human brain, neurotransmitters are the most important for moment-to-moment operations of the brain, because they carry the message of one nerve cell to another, as would a courier, across the cleft (technically called *synapse*) between the nerve cells. Every stimulus that our sensory organs receive, every thought that crosses our mind, every emotion that we feel stirs up this sea of neurotransmitters. Therefore, if a disorder occurs because of the deficiency or malfunction of a particular neurotransmitter, its rational treatment should include administering the neurotransmitter or medicines that increase its availability and reception at the synaptic cleft. That is exactly what the medications for ADD purport to do.

First-line medications: The first line of chemical defense against ADD is a group of medications called *psychostimulants*, a misnomer that has caused much misgiving in the lay press. These medications work in areas of the brain—such as the prefrontal cortex—that regulate attention, releasing dopamine from nerve cells and preventing its reuptake by the cells; thus increasing the levels of dopamine in the cleft between nerve cells. The foremost among the psychostimulants is methylphenidate (sold under the brand name of Ritalin by the drug company Ciba-Geigy, now Novartis), the most commonly prescribed medication for ADD. The others include the various salts of dextroamphetamine (sold as Dexedrine, Adderall, or Dextrostat) and pemoline sodium (sold as Cylert).

• **Methylphenidate (Ritalin).** This drug was approved by the Federal Drug Administration (FDA) in 1955 under the brand name Ritalin for the pharmaceutical company Ciba-Geigy, now Novartis. Ciba-Geigy's patent expired in 1996, and now many companies make the generic form of the drug. Methylphenidate is available as 5-, 10-, and 20-mg tablets. Long-acting tablets are available in 20-mg strength as sustained-release (SR) tablets and in 10-, 18-, 20-, and 36-mg extended-release tablets. A liquid form is not available. The regular form acts only for four hours, while the sustained-release form acts from six to eight hours. The tablet should be swallowed whole and should preferably be taken thirty minutes before eating. Although pharmacists caution not to divide the tablet, no significant loss of potency occurs if it is. Similarly, no substantial loss of potency occurs if the medication is taken with or after food. Although the FDA does not approve the use of methylphenidate for children under the age of six years old, this caution simply means that data substantiating the effectiveness and safety of Ritalin are not available in children below the age of six years old. The Federal Drug and Cosmetic Act does not limit the manner in which a physician uses it. In fact, Ritalin has been given to children as young as four years old without any problems. Nonetheless, be sure to discuss this with your child's pediatrician.

Unlike other pediatric medications, methylphenidate is not given on a weight basis. Usually a 5-mg dose is started two or three times a day, and is increased by 5-mg every third day, depending on the response and side effects. The usual dose is 0.3-0.5 mg/kg/day. Higher doses are required for the hyperactive type of ADD, whereas children with the inattentive type of ADD respond to lower doses. Doses higher than 1 mg/kg/day are counterproductive because side effects increase at such doses without further benefits. Therefore, more is not necessarily better. Blood levels are not required. Ritalin should be given cautiously to children who are hypersensitive to it, or to those with psychosis, anxiety, agitation, tics, seizures, and cardiovascular disease. Foods rich in tyramine—such as chocolate, bologna, pepperoni, caffeine, and canned fish—should not be given to a child who is receiving methylphenidate. The effects of medication should be monitored with questionnaires.

Side-effects hysteria—is it justified? Contrary to the frenetic propaganda of the anti-Ritalin lobby, methylphenidate is a safe medication. Russell Barkley, a nationally renowned researcher in the field of ADD, reported in 1990 that, out of eighty-three school-age children who received Ritalin, only three had to discontinue it because of side effects. Seventeen side effects alleged to be associated with the administration of Ritalin were meticulously monitored by parents in this study, using a zero-to-nine rating scale. Similar results have been reported for preschool children. Researchers at the University of Ottawa, Ontario, Canada, noted, in cognitive tests, improvements in attention and reduction of impulsivity with methylphenidate in preschool children. The children's ability to work more productively also showed improvement.

Passions against Ritalin are also abetted by the long list of adverse effects given in the *Physician's Desk Reference* (*PDR*). This document, published by the Medical Economics Company in collaboration with drug manufacturers, is now widely available to practitioners and consumers through the Internet and provides an "exact copy of the product's government-approved labeling" for all prescription drugs available on the market. The Code of Federal Regulations further requires that "any relevant warnings, hazards, contraindications, side effects, and precautions" be included in the *PDR* content and must be the "same in language and emphasis" as the product label that has been approved. Because the intent of the law is to inform the consumer of all possible adverse effects—even if they are infrequent—the cautions and side effects listed in the *PDR* can be alarming. However, one should compare the frequency of side effects in those receiving the medication with the frequency of side effects in a similar group of individuals not receiving the medication. If an adverse effect occurs more frequently in those taking a particular medication, only then should it be attributed to the medication. Every association is not causal. Many of the side effects reported to the FDA's Spontaneous Reporting System can occur by chance and not necessarily due to Ritalin. Many of the adverse effects of Ritalin listed in the PDR are very infrequent and cause minuscule inconvenience as compared with the pervasive dysfunction that ADD causes. Or, in other words, the risks of taking Ritalin are much smaller than the benefit that accrues from it.

According to the *PDR*, the possible side effects of Ritalin include loss of appetite, difficulty in sleeping (insomnia), headache, stomachache, tics, agitation, dizziness, sadness (melancholia), unhappiness (dysphoria), proneness to crying, decreased linear growth, abdominal pain, palpitations, increase of heart rate and blood pressure, skin rashes and itching, and weight loss. However, only appetite suppression, lack of sleep, stomachache, headache, and dizziness are reported to occur more often in those receiving methyphenidate as compared with those not receiving it. Rebound effects—such as, ravenous appetite and irritability—which occur as the effect of the drug wanes in the evenings, can be controlled by adjusting the frequency and dose of the medication. Stomachaches and headaches are temporary and decrease after a few days. The effect on appetite can be mitigated by administering methylphenidate with or after food. Insomnia does not occur if the medicine is not administered in late evening.

According to a group of researchers at the Royal Children's Hospital, Melbourne, Australia, many of the alleged side effects are indeed "preexisting characteristics of children with ADHD." Similarly researchers at the University of British Columbia, Vancouver, Canada, found that many side effects reported by parents and teachers are similar to the symptoms of ADD.

Palpitations and increased blood pressure are so uncommon in therapeutic doses that the American Heart Association in its seventy-first session in Boston, Massachusetts, declared that no cardiac monitoring is required for Ritalin. Intravenous injection of high doses of methylphenidate in experimental animals has been reported to produce a few microscopic changes in the heart muscle, but the clinical significance of these changes is unknown.

No, Ritalin does not make children zombies. The fear that methylphenidate will make a child a zombie is absolutely baseless. Methylphenidate neither causes drowsiness nor decreases mental abilities. Researchers at McGill University in Canada reported a positive effect of methylphenidate on measures of mental flexibility and problem-solving abilities. A very small fraction of children taking Ritalin appear sad and cry excessively. Obviously, such children are not suitable candidates for Ritalin.

No, Ritalin does not cause "robotic conformity." A child taking Ritalin follows class rules rather than his impulses. This improves his academic performance and social behavior. Whereas a child with ADD constantly craves reinforcement and approval, the effort of a child receiving Ritalin becomes goal-directed and independent of rewards. Methylphenidate improves persistence by enhancing the processes that maintain effort over time. Yes, a child taking Ritalin loses unproductive spontaneity—spontaneity that disrupts others and interferes with his own goals. And, yes, he conforms to societal rules. But he does not become a robot, a mindless creature that just follows orders.

Ritalin and cancer. Ciba-Geigy (now Novartis), the pharmaceutical company that patented Ritalin, conducted trials on animals and found no evidence that Ritalin causes cancer, even if it was used for long periods of time. Researchers at the National Institute of Environmental Health Sciences administered a wide range of methylphenidate doses to rats and mice over a number of years, but did not find any increase in cancers in rats. In fact, they reported less than the expected rate of cancers in rats taking methylphenidate. However, a slight increase in benign tumors of the liver and increased liver weights was observed in mice at a high dose. An increase in hepatoblastomas was also seen in high-dose male mice. Such high doses are rarely used to treat ADD. The authors concluded that "epidemiologic studies of methylphenidate have found no evidence of a carcinogenic effect in humans and like our findings in rats, report a less than expected rate of cancers in patients taking methylphenidate."

Ritalin and tics. It is generally believed that methylphenidate can induce muscle twitches and spasms, called tics. Tics result in sudden blinking, jerking of the hands or shrugging of the shoulders, or making faces. However, this happens only in those children who have a history of tics or whose families have another member who has tics. In other words, Ritalin can induce a latent tendency for tics, but it does not induce tics in those who do not have a predisposition to them. In fact, in children in whom tics were due to hyperactivity, methylphenidate actually improved tics. Researchers at the Hospital for Sick Children in Toronto, Canada, found that Ritalin did not precipitate or exacerbate tics.

Ritalin is not "speed." The misnomer "psychostimulant" perpetuates a myth that Ritalin is an amphetamine—or speed. Chemically, Ritalin (methylphenidate) is a piperidine, whereas amphetamine is methylphenethylamine. In the doses prescribed by physicians, methylphenidate does not cause euphoria or enhance performance. Calling Ritalin "kiddie cocaine" is hyperbole. However, the problems and risks mount significantly when Ritalin is abused by taking it in high doses and through abnormal routes. Problems associated with the abusive use of methylphenidate are described in a later section of the book.

Ritalin and suppression of growth. The issue of growth suppression by methylphenidate was examined by researchers at the

Massachusetts General Hospital, in Boston. The growth of 124 children with ADD was compared with that of 109 controls. A small difference in height was noted between the ADD and non-ADD children through mid-adolescence, but it was unrelated to the use of methylphenidate. Moreover, by late adolescence this difference disappeared. Dr. Peter R. Breggin, author of *Talking Back to Ritalin*—in which he suggests that Ritalin suppresses growth—contradicts himself by citing Yudofsky and colleagues, who, according to him, admit that growth lag induced by Ritalin is temporary "in most cases."

A multicenter study group sponsored by the National Institute of Mental Health has concluded that methylphenidate is superior to psychosocial interventions in simple ADD. The study included 579 children between the ages of seven and nine years at six medical centers across the U. S. and Canada: New York State Psychiatric Institute, Duke University, University of California (in Berkeley and in Irvine), University of Pittsburgh, and McGill University (Montreal, Canada). The study is being hailed as a landmark that, according to Dr. James T. McCracken, the director of child and adolescent psychiatry at the Neuropsychiatric Institute of the University of California at Los Angeles, should put the Ritalin controversy to rest. Methylphenidate and dextroamphetamine are the safest and most effective treatments for ADD. Dextroamphetamine has been used for over fifty years and Ritalin for over forty years, both without significant long-term adverse effects.

Caution should be exercised in giving methylphenidate with other drugs, because it may interfere with their metabolism in the body. This principle applies not only to methylphenidate, but to medications in general. Drugs use similar channels for their degradation and elimination from the body and may compete with one another for these if administered together. Methylphenidate decreases the elimination of antiepileptics, antidepressants, anticoagulants—such as coumadin and phenylbutazone—and may increase their levels in the blood if given with them. Doses of such medications should, therefore, be decreased when these are given along with methylphenidate. Methylphenidate can also interact with anesthetic agents. Parents should inform the anesthesiologist before surgery that their child is taking methylphenidate. Methylphenidate should not be given if a child has glaucoma (an eye disease characterized by increased eye pressure), severe anxiety, or complaints of hallucinations (seeing and hearing things that are not present).

• **Amphetamines:** Dextroamphetamine, the most popular form of therapeutic amphetamine, is available under the brand names Dexedrine, Dextrostat, and Adderall. Dexedrine is available as a 5-, 10-, 15-mg sustained-release spansule (a special type of capsule in which the initial dose is released as the capsule is taken, and the rest of the dose is released slowly over a prolonged period of time), and as an elixir (rarely stocked by pharmacists). Dextrostat is available as 5- and 10-mg tablets. Dextroamphetamine tablets can be crushed and mixed with apple sauce, but should not be chewed. Sustained-release capsules should be swallowed whole. Amphetamines should not be taken with fruit juice. Dextroamphetamine spansules and Adderall act longer than methylphenidate—for about six to eight hours—whereas the regular tablets and elixir of dextroamphetamine, like methylphenidate, act for three to four hours. Adderall is a mixture of four salts, combined to decrease toxicity and increase the duration of effect. It is available in 5-, 10-, 15-, and 20-mg tablets. The tablets have two lines debossed in them (double scored) and can be easily divided to adjust the dose. Dextroamphetamine is not recommended for children under the age of three.

For children under six years of age, treatment should be started with 2.5-mg of dextroamphetamine daily and should be increased by 2.5-mg/day at weekly intervals. For children older than six years, the initial dose is 5-mg/day, increased by 5-mg at weekly intervals. The daily dose should not exceed a total of 45-mg in three divided doses. For a long-lasting effect, a spansule can be given in one daily dose.

Side effects include palpitations, tachycardia, increase in blood pressure, exacerbation of tics, restlessness, insomnia, psychotic episodes (rarely), dryness of mouth, loss of appetite, and weight loss.

A less-popular amphetamine, methamphetamine, is also available to treat ADD as 5-mg tablets under the brand name Desoxyn. Its effects and side effects are similar to those of dextroamphetamine in all other aspects.

 • **Pemoline sulfate (Cylert):** This medication offers the convenience of once-a-day dosing, because it acts for six to eight hours. An additional advantage for practitioners is that it does not have to be prescribed as a controlled substance. It is available as 18.75-, 37.5-, and 75-mg regular tablets and 37.5-mg chewable tablets. An FDA advisory includes that it is not recommended for children under six. The starting dose is a 37.5-mg single dose each morning, to be increased by 18.75 mg/week. The effective dose is 56.25- to 75-mg, not to exceed 112.5-mg/day.

Adverse effects include liver dysfunction and failure, decreased seizure threshold, depression of the bone marrow resulting in anemia and low white blood cells, hallucinations, abnormal movements of the tongue, loss of appetite, weight loss, and nausea. The pediatrician should always do a blood test for liver function before giving pemoline, and should repeat the test if the child complains of nausea, vomiting, and pain in the belly.

To avoid nervousness, caffeine-rich foods—such as iced tea, chocolate, coffee, and certain sodas—should be avoided or used in moderation when a child is taking psychostimulants. The psychostimulants should not be prescribed if more serious psychiatric diseases—such as juvenile mania or psychosis—are suspected.

Second-line medications: What if psychostimulants do not work or children cannot take them because of intolerable side effects? In such cases, one of the following medications—either alone or in combination with the sychostimulants—may be required. Children who have psychiatric symptoms—such as anxiety and depression—in addition to ADD, may also require the following medications. I have called them "second line" because they are usually not the first choice in the treatment of ADD.

 • **Clonidine (Catapres):** A medication used to treat hypertension in adults, clonidine is useful in ADD because it inhibits the activity of receptors that produce the neurotransmitter noradrenaline in an area of the brain called the locus ceruleus. It is available as 0.1-, 0.2-, or 0.3-mg tablets and as a patch to be applied on the skin (transdermal) once a week to deliver 0.1-, 0.2-, or 0.3-mg of clonidine per day for seven days. It is especially useful if the child has a tic disorder, Tourette's syndrome, and difficulty sleeping at night, and is hyperactive, oppositional, or aggressive. It is particularly helpful if a child presents with difficulties in the morning. Side effects of clonidine include drowsiness, dry mouth, sudden fall of blood pressure on standing (orthostatic hypotension), nausea, vomiting, depression, and skin rash. It is usually begun at a dose of 0.05-mg and given at bedtime because it has a sedative effect, and is increased gradually over two to three weeks, in three or four divided doses, up to 3- to 6-microgram/kg/day.

Tenex or guanfacine, available as 1- and 2-mg tablets, is a similar medication, but has less side effects because it acts more selectively on the noradrenergic receptors.

Because of the potential for adverse effects on the cardiovascular system, the following precautions should be taken while administering clonidine and guanfacine, especially, in combination with psychostimulants:

- Children with significant heart disease should not take clonidine;
- Children with a history of syncope (sudden fainting) and low heart rate should be seen by a cardiologist before clonidine is prescribed;
- Children with diseases of the kidney should not receive clonidine if they have high blood pressure;
- Pulse rate and blood pressure should be monitored before beginning treatment weekly as the dose is being adjusted, and then every four to six weeks during maintenance. If the pulse is less than 60 beats/minute, or if the blood pressure is low or high, the child should be seen by a cardiologist;
- If a child develops symptoms such as dizziness, fatigue, lightheadedness, drowsiness, and fainting—especially if these symptoms occur with exercise—he should see his doctor immediately;
- Blood pressure should remain between 80- and 140-mm of Hg;
- Do not stop clonidine abruptly, because sudden withdrawal of clonidine can cause a sudden rise in blood pressure.

Although a few fatalities have been reported in children who were administered a combination of clonidine and Ritalin, most of these children had preexisting heart disease and the above precautions were not observed.

• **Antiseizure medications—carbamazepine (Tegretol) or valproic acid (Depakene):** These two antiseizure medications are often prescribed by psychiatrists to control hyperactive, aggressive, and maniacal behavior, especially in children with a history of brain injury even if these children do not have seizures. Antiseizure medications have more serious side effects than methylphenidate and should be prescribed with caution and monitored carefully.

• **Antidepressants:** Children, especially adolescents with ADD, frequently have anxiety and depression. Tricyclic antidepressants—such as amitriptyline, imipramine, and desipramine—can be used to manage both of these symptoms in such patients. Tricyclic antidepressants inhibit reuptake of both dopamine and noradrenaline by the nerve cells, increasing the levels of both in the synapse. Once again, they are much more toxic than methylphenidate and should be used cautiously in children with cardiac dysfunction. Blood counts (CBC), blood levels, liver enzymes, and electrocardiogram (EKG) should be obtained periodically to monitor their side effects. These include drowsiness, incoordination, blurred vision, dry mouth, insomnia, anxiety, confusion, delusion, and psychosis.

• **Newer antidepressants (the famous—or infamous—Prozac):** The newer antidepressants belonging to the class of serotonin reuptake inhibitors—such as Prozac, Paxil, Luvox, and Zoloft—are safer than tricyclics. These are useful for treating ADD complicated by anxiety, panic disorder, social phobia, and bulimia. So far, they have been used more often in adults with ADD than in children with ADD.

Third-line medications (if everything else fails): Children with mental retardation and autism often do not respond to methylphenidate and other medications mentioned above. If such children manifest abnormal and challenging behaviors, neuroleptics (medicines used to treat psychosis, such as schizophrenia) may be required to manage them. Once again, medications should not be used in isolation, but in concert with a program of behavior management. Neuroleptics inhibit many types of nerve cell receptors and, therefore, have more side effects than the medications described above. These should be prescribed only by psychiatrists who specialize in treating children with disabling conditions.

• **Thioridazine (Mellaril):** Once, Mellaril was the most frequently used medicine to quiet an aggressive and uncontrollable child with mental retardation, but it has fallen into disrepute because of its side effects and the availability of better alternatives. Adverse effects include sudden stiffening of the body with or without upturning of the eyes (extrapyramidal movement disorder), high fever (neuroleptic malignant syndrome), drowsiness, restlessness, nausea, blurred vision, dry mouth, weight gain, or weight loss. Long-term use can result in a constellation of abnormal movements called tardive dyskinesia. These include rolling and thrusting of the tongue, sucking and smacking of the lips, facial grimacing, sudden arm flinging or hand writhing, abnormal posturing of the body, and tics. Some children have similar movements when the drug is withdrawn. Tardive dyskinesia may or may not disappear upon withdrawal of medication.

• **Haloperidol (Haldol):** A neuroleptic once considered specific for autism, haloperidol is also used less frequently nowadays because of serious side effects and better alternatives. Cautions and side effects are the same as in thioridazine.

• **Risperidone (Risperdal):** A newer antipsychotic medication, risperidone has fewer side effects than haloperidol and is less sedative. At least two studies have reported that it improves severe aggressive behavior and temper outbursts in children with autism. Its improved efficacy is due to its effects on serotonin as well as dopamine receptors.

SUMMARY

Because of the stringent regulatory requirements for the medications described above to be approved for specific diseases, only three are formally approved by the FDA as treatments of ADD: methylphenidate, dextroamphetamine, and pemoline. This does not mean that off-label medications cannot be used by physicians to treat ADD. However, the physicians should inform parents about such off-label use. Because of the side-effect hysteria, a few physicians obtain consent from parents to use psychostimulants in children. I think this act legitimizes the intimidating propaganda of the anti-Ritalin lobby, as if prescribing Ritalin were a highly risky medical procedure. I do not take written consents before I prescribe psychostimulants, because the risks are no higher than those of antibiotics.

I have described these medications not to intimidate readers pedagogically—or to turn them into self-treating patients—but to underscore the hype about methylphenidate (Ritalin). Of all the medications described above, methylphenidate is the safest and the least toxic—yet the most maligned—medication. Unlike methylphenidate, many of the above medications leave permanent sequelae, such as tardive dyskinesia, and a few, such as desipramine, can have fatal cardiac consequences.

Although methylphenidate is safer than almost all of the other medications described above, it is classified as a Schedule II Controlled Substance and requires a special prescription in most states, through which the states can track its use. I hope that discerning parents will be able to make informed choices among medications when they, their child, and their child's physician have decided that medication is the road they want to take.

21

Will My Child Get Addicted to Ritalin?

Ritalin (methylphenidate)—like amphetamines and cocaine—works on the neurotransmitter dopamine, activating the brainstem arousal system and cortex; but it has low addictive potential because it crosses the blood-brain barrier more slowly than amphetamines and cocain. According to a study published in the *American Journal of Psychiatry* by Dr. Nora Volkow, chair of the medical department at Brookhaven National Laboratory, in New York, methylphenidate crosses the blood-brain barrier over a period of one hour after a standard dose; thus not giving the pleasurable high that is associated with and responsible for cocaine addiction. It differs from cocaine in its clearance from the brain tissues as well—clearance of methylphenidate being significantly slower than that of cocaine.

Webster's Dictionary defines addiction as a habit or practice whose cessation causes severe trauma. Cessation of Ritalin does not cause severe trauma, although a rebound of symptoms may occur. If used properly under supervision, Ritalin is not addictive, although there is a slight risk of developing a psychological dependence on it, even when it is taken according to the prescribed directions. Parents and their child learn to associate Ritalin with good behavior and better academic performance. They can become very apprehensive when the physician recommends that they should stop Ritalin to see if the child has outgrown ADD. This psychological dependence actually validates the fact that Ritalin made such a salutary difference in their lives that they come to regard it as their savior. The phenomenon of tolerance—or a decrease in the effect of Ritalin with time—has been noted with the sustained-release form of Ritalin. Once again, this decrement in therapeutic effect is not associated with the emergence of new symptoms of drug withdrawal.

According to Dr. Cooper, associate director for Medical Affairs at the National Institute of Drug Abuse, in Rockville, Maryland, there is a low level of methylphenidate abuse among high school students, though the number of high school students taking Ritalin without prescription has decreased in recent years. Drug abuse is as much a function of the drug as it is of the person who abuses it. Ritalin abuse is not inherent in Ritalin, but in the person who uses it. Individuals prone to drug addiction get addicted even to painkillers. The *Physician's Desk Reference* (*PDR*) advises that "Ritalin should be given cautiously to emotionally unstable patients, such as those with a history of drug dependence and alcoholism, because such patients may increase the dosage on their own initiative." Caution should be used in prescribing, dispensing, and storing Ritalin so that every tablet is accounted for. However, to condemn it lock, stock and barrel is foolhardy, because adolescents and young adults with untreated ADD are much more likely to become drug addicts than their non-ADD counterparts.

The physician should be on the lookout for symptoms caused by excessive doses of methylphenidate. High doses of stimulants produce a predictable set of symptoms: tremors and muscle twitching; fevers, convulsions, and headaches (which may be severe); and irregular heartbeat and respirations (which may be profound and life-threatening). Loss of appetite may result in serious malnutrition. Chronically abusive use can lead to marked tolerance and psychic dependence with varying degrees of abnormal behaviors—such as anxiety, restlessness, excessive repetition of movements and meaningless tasks, formication (sensation of bugs or worms crawling under the skin), paranoia, hallucinations, and delusions (toxic psychosis). Psychotic episodes can occur, especially with intravenous abuse. Careful supervision is required during drug withdrawal, because severe depression—as well as the effects of chronic overactivity—can be unmasked. Long-term follow-up may be required because of the patient's underlying personality disturbances.

Methylphenidate tablets—which produce mild stimulant effects when taken as directed and at the usual prescription doses—can create powerful cocaine-like stimulant effects and serious health risks when crushed and snorted like cocaine or injected intravenously like heroin. Therapeutically, Ritalin is intended only for oral use, but many nonmedical users crush the tablets and either snort the resulting powder or dissolve it in water and "cook" it for intravenous injection. An unsophisticated street user may prepare the drug unhygienically, introducing dust, dirt, bacteria, pollen, talc, lint, and other contaminants into the liquid prepared for injection. The "inert ingredients"—called excipients—included by manufacturers to increase the bulk of the tablets may be harmless when taken by mouth, but can create serious problems when injected directly into veins or body tissues. In order to make the 5- to 20-mg tablets large enough to be handled easily—depending on size, formulation, and the manufacturer—at least 100-mg of inert ingredients—such as lactose, starch, polyethelene glycol, magnesium stearate, sucrose, talc, cellulose, mineral oil, and various dyes and conditioning agents—are found in Ritalin tablets. Although these ingredients are "inert" when taken by mouth, they can cause serious problems when injected or snorted. The rapid delivery of drugs via injection makes it difficult for the user to control the intensity of the drug effect; thus making toxic overdoses more likely. There are numerous reports in medical journals about permanent and irreversible lung tissue damage related to injection of crushed Ritalin tablets.

Snorting (intranasal insufflation) of Ritalin damages the delicate epithelial tissues that line the nasal cavities and air passages. Ritalin tablets contain the hydrochloride salt of methylphenidate and yield dilute hydrochloric acid when they come into contact with moisture. Although this is not a problem in the stomach (hydrochloric acid is one of the digestive acids produced in the stomach), in the nasal passages the acid can "burn" the delicate nasal tissues, resulting in open sores, nose bleeds, and possibly deterioration of the nasal cartilage. While death due to the nonmedical use of Ritalin is not common, it has been known to occur.

Ritalin (methylphenidate) and dextroamphetamine are Schedule II Controlled Substances under both the federal and most states' Controlled Substances Acts. Schedule II drugs are covered by strict manufacturing quotas, careful inventory controls, and separate record-keeping requirements. Prescriptions may not be refilled—a new prescription is required for additional supplies. Prescriptions must be in writing and limited to an amount sufficient for one month plus one week, if used in accordance with the prescribing instructions. In many states, the prescription should be written on a special, numbered, three-part prescription form obtained from the state Drug Enforcement Agency (DEA) by special order. Thus, these drugs are tightly regulated, from the manufacturer to the patient.

Under both federal and state law, dealing in or distributing Ritalin is a serious felony. Depending on the quantity, location of transfer, and age of the recipient, dealing in Ritalin could be a Class A felony resulting in a prison term and fine, which differ state by state, but can be as great as forty-five years and $10,000 (under Indiana law). In Indiana, even possession of Ritalin without a prescription is a felony. There are increased penalties for dealing it to minors under age eighteen, or dealing on or within 1,000 feet of school property or a school bus, or near public parks.

In recent years, the frequency of diagnosis for ADD has increased dramatically, especially because adults are now diagnosed with this disorder—previously considered a children-only disease. Prescriptions for Ritalin have increased more than 600 percent over the past five years according to the DEA. In the United States, about 1.5 million (2.8 percent) of children ages five-to-eighteen years were receiving methylphenidate in mid-1995. Despite an astronomical increase in the diagnosis of ADD over the past several years, manufacturing quotas have not increased sufficiently to allow for the increased demand. This has led to sporadic and regional shortages of Ritalin, and a significant portion of these prescriptions are being diverted for illicit nonmedical use. Diversion of drugs into the illicit street drug trade increases the shortages of the drug for legitimate medical purposes. When purchased in pharmacies with a valid prescription, Ritalin tablets usually cost twenty-five to fifty cents each. In the illicit street drug market, tablets sell for $3 to $1—each as "vitamin R," "R-Ball," or the "Smart Drug."

Despite the legal and medical safeguards mentioned above, the nonmedical use of Ritalin is on the rise and has been the subject of numerous television specials and news magazine articles. At a December 1994 meeting of the Community Epidemiology Work Group—a drug-use epidemiology forum—an upsurge in illicit street use of Ritalin was reported in the United States on the West Coast and in the Midwest. Anecdotal reports suggest that suburban and white abusers are somewhat more likely to snort Ritalin, whereas black inner-city abusers are somewhat more likely to inject it.

Of the studies about the role of Ritalin in drug abuse, most have concluded that drug therapy of children with ADD is protective against substance abuse. Dr. Timothy Wilens—a psychiatrist at Massachusetts General Hospital, Boston, who followed 500 children—found lower rates of drug abuse among medicated children with ADD than in the unmedicated group with ADD. Similarly, a psychologist, Jan Loney, at the State University of New York at Stony Brook— who tracked 300 children diagnosed with ADD in the 1960s and 1970s—found that children with ADD who were on medications were less likely to be using drugs. There is only one study on the other side of this debate, by Nadine

Lambert, a professor of education at University of California at Berkeley, who contends that exposure to Ritalin makes the brain more susceptible to drug abuse. Professor Lambert's conclusions are based on the follow-up of 500 children with severe ADD for over twenty-six years. However, her critics argue that children in her cohort had severe ADD which predisposes them to drug abuse anyway.

"Drugging Unruly Kids Lazy Parents' Cop-out."
Headline: "Plain Talk" column—AL NEUHARTH
USA Today, *December 19, 1999*

22

Is Ritalin a Panacea for All the Ills of Children?
WHEN USING RITALIN IS NOT WARRANTED

Medicinal drugs are double-edged swords. If used judiciously, they give relief; if used improperly, they cause damage. When used at an appropriate dose under medical supervision, Ritalin decreases hyperactivity and increases attention span, resulting in better academic and social skills. But if used unnecessarily, Ritalin (as well as its generic cousins) is useless and can be harmful.

Those ingesting Ritalin unnecessarily fall into two general categories: those who are wrongly diagnosed to have ADD, and those (usually teenagers) who use it as a recreational drug. The diagnosis and treatment of ADD are as much an art as a science. It is not backed up by blood work, MRI, or x-rays. There is no blood work or screening test to determine which patients would benefit from Ritalin. Therefore, it is easy for parents and teachers to make a pitch for ADD when they want to enhance a child's performance or to make the work of parenting and teaching easier. To make matters worse, Ritalin produces a few positive effects in individuals without ADD, as well. This complicates the work of doctors nationwide, who are under constant pressure to prescribe Ritalin when not indicated and under constant criticism if they prescribe Ritalin when it is indicated. Some of the situations in which Ritalin is given unnecessarily are described below.

Ritalin as a sedative: Many experts are critical of what they describe as the use of Ritalin as a "quick fix" by impatient, haggard parents to calm their rambunctious children. In addition, these critics warn, there have been no long-term studies to determine if Ritalin is harmful when administered to individuals without ADD. According to Dr. Peter S. Jensen, chief of the Child and Adolescent Disorders Research Branch of the National Institute of Mental Health, Ritalin is overprescribed. He says, "I fear that ADHD is suffering from the 'disease of the month' syndrome." He also notes that even teachers of preschool children are known to suggest Ritalin to parents of active kids. Psychiatrists nationwide often feel immense pressure to prescribe Ritalin, and sometimes after only a very brief examination.

Ritalin as a study aid: Ritalin is abused by some teenagers and young adults as a "study aid," to improve classroom performance and performance before examinations. According to some high school juniors, taking a few pills of Ritalin is like drinking a few cups of coffee to stay up all night, because it helps them to concentrate, think, and study better. But, like a few cups of coffee, it can cause overexcitement, a state in which one is wide awake, anxiously trying to memorize as much information as possible. Although such a person may be able to scan more material, such hurriedly gathered information is not retained well. Ritalin can also result in an overfocused state in which the child obsesses about a few aspects of the study material, neglecting others. The use of Ritalin as a study aid is, thus, counterproductive, resulting in poor performance.

Ritalin as performance enhancer: Some teachers are quick to consider the possibility of ADD if a student is not doing well in class. Children who cannot keep pace with the class work often tune out and appear inattentive. Ritalin should not be administered to such children solely with the intention of boosting their performance in the classroom. Ritalin does not change a child's innate learning style, nor does it improve intelligence. It does not lead to the spontaneous acquisition of new skills. Its effects on academic achievement are mediated by improved attention span, motor inhibition, and inhibition of the flight of ideas. Therefore, if a child's poor performance is due to learning disability or poor intelligence, Ritalin is unlikely to help.

Ritalin as a social restraint: According to Peter Breggin, author of *Toxic Psychiatry* and the bestselling *Talking Back to Prozac,* Ritalin is a "method of social control of children." Some parents want their child to take this drug so that they can make it through the day. Ritalin should not be used as a baby-sitting aid for a lively energetic youngster because it will decrease his curiosity and drive to learn.

Parenting is a tough job. It involves motivating children to perform and regulating them when they overshoot the mark. Ritalin should not be used just to facilitate the job of parenting, because it can inhibit the development of self-control in the child. Children will have an easy excuse to misbehave if they do not get the medication, conditioning both parents and children to think that they cannot function without the medication—a state of psychological dependence. Therefore, I recommend that medication should be discontinued during the summer (medication holiday), even in a properly diagnosed child, to see if the child has learned to control her or himself.

Ritalin as a smoke screen: Ritalin should not be used to hide more serious problems in the child and the family. As I have discussed in the section on differential diagnosis (Chapter 14, "Does Everyone Who Moves Have ADD?"), symptoms mimicking ADD can occur in a variety of conditions. Parents with unresolved psychic and marital conflicts often project their problems onto one target child who may simply be reacting to the psychic disequilibrium at home. Depressed mothers often blame their children for their predicament and plead for medication. A few parents deny the low endowment of their learning-disabled or mentally retarded child and find it more acceptable to have him or her labeled as "hyper," whereas the child may be responding to pressures to achieve.

A thorough history and evaluation are essential to exclude these masqueraders. (See the chapters on diagnosis—Chapter 9, "How is ADD Diagnosed?"—and differential diagnosis—Chapter 14, "Does Everyone Who Moves Have ADD?")

"If sack and sugar be a fault, God help the wicked!"

SHAKESPEARE
King Henry IV

23

Is ADD Caused by Sugar, Dyes, or Salicylates?

Food and health are inextricably interwoven in folklore. We are but what we eat, says the ancient Indian science of Ayurveda. People have been looking at food as a source of health as well as of disease since time immemorial. Hippocrates, who is supposed by many to be the father of modern medicine, believed that diseases were caused by vapors that formed from the residue of undesirable diet. Whereas there is credible evidence that certain dietary habits cause physical diseases such as heart disease and colon cancer, the relation between diet and behavior is far from proven. Sugar, dyes, and salicylates are often incriminated as causes of hyperactivity. In this chapter, I have tried to present whatever evidence we have about the role of these substances in the causation of ADD.

Sugar: Contrary to popular belief, nutritive sweeteners—such as refined sugars and corn syrup—have little effect on behavior. At least twelve research studies performed under controlled conditions have shown that sugar and artificial sweeteners do not cause ADD or increase its symptoms. The activity and attention of twenty-one boys alleged to be responders to restriction of sugar were assessed objectively by a group of researchers after challenging the boys with glucose and sucrose. These researchers found that the motor activity of these children actually decreased after the sugar challenge. Another group of researchers compared the effect of sucrose with that of an equivalent amount of aspartame in children, ages four and five. They did not notice any effect of sucrose on a child's activity level and attentiveness in play situations or learning tasks. A third group of researchers studied fourteen boys with ADD, ages two to six years old, who were referred to them because their parents believed that they responded to sugar restriction. These children were observed by their parents subjectively and by using an actometer over a four-day period under four different conditions: 1.75 g/kg sucrose, glucose, aspartame, and saccharin. An actometer is a watch-like gadget that measures the physical movements of children. No differences were noticed under any of these conditions.

A team of researchers led by Mark Wolraich at Vanderbilt University, Nashville, Tennessee, gave diets containing saccharin, sucrose, or aspartame in a double-blind manner for three weeks to forty-eight children who were described by their parents as sugar-sensitive. (Double-blind means that neither the person who administers the medication, nor the one who measures the outcome, knows what the child is taking, ensuring an unbiased measurement of outcome.) They found no difference in thirty-nine measures of intelligence and behavior among the three groups. After a review of sixteen studies about the effect of nutritional sweeteners on attention and activity, Wolraich and his colleagues concluded that the overall effect was not significant. Most studies had limitations: they involved small samples; children were often recruited through advertisements looking for children whose parents thought them to be sugar responsive, thus were likely to be more severely impaired; instruments used to measure outcome are not considered to be specific or sensitive, and are generally not used in clinical practice; and measurements were not made under natural conditions.

Despite the lack of evidence in scientific studies for a causal role for sugar in ADD, sugar as a cause of hyperactivity is deeply ingrained in the public's mind. More than eighty-nine percent of Canadian primary school teachers—in a study conducted at Brock University, Canada—believed that sugar contributes to hyperactivity and behavioral problems in children. More than half of the teachers had counseled parents of children with hyperactivity to reduce the sugar consumption of their children. I do not argue with parents who firmly believe in this myth, because decreasing sugar consumption does not harm children. In fact, eating too much candy is harmful for teeth and weight, anyway. However, if restriction of sugar becomes a food fad and results in tremendous parent/child conflict, I do caution parents that there is no evidence that sugar causes hyperactivity.

Salicylate and dyes: Dr. Ben F. Feingold created a sensation in the 1970s by hypothesizing that children with ADD may be helped by removing from their diets synthetic colors and flavors, as well as natural foods containing salicylates, such as oranges, apples, cucumbers, and tomatoes ("Feingold hypothesis"). His book *Why Your Child Is Hyperactive* became a bestseller. Dr. Feingold, as the chief allergist at the Kaiser Medical Care Program in northern California, was an expert on salicylate sensitivity. His life-long interest in ADD began when he fortuitously cured a woman's aggressive and hostile behavior while treating her giant hives with an elimination diet. Constant irritation and itching associated with hives can frustrate and annoy even the most stoic person—it is like having ants all over the body. Perhaps this woman's hives were the cause of her hostility and annoyance. He later observed positive behavioral changes among several of his patients with food allergies when he introduced diets free of artificial colors and substances, salicylates, and all naturally-occurring fruits and vegetables that contain molecules resembling salicylate. He collected these anecdotal reports to support his hypothesis.

Feingold's diet involved the elimination of almost anything that children hold dear. Let me give you a taste of it: no tomatoes, berries, cherries, grapes, nectarines, oranges, peaches, instant breakfast cereals, manufactured cakes, cookies, doughnuts, pies, bologna, salami, sausages, frankfurters, barbecued poultry, flavored yogurt, toothpastes, candies, or chocolates. Such a dietary regime would require meticulous twenty-four-hour-a-day monitoring of children's diet by their parents. This one-on-one monitoring by parents would involve some form of refocusing of their child that would ameliorate the symptoms of ADD. Moreover, if the child were truly allergic, relief of the symptoms of allergy would make him less irritable and agitated.

Dr. Feingold's hypothesis has not been proved in research studies. A group of researchers studied the effect of artificial coloring on behavior in a double-blind crossover study in twenty-two children. (Crossover means that every child receives sequentially both the treatment and the placebo, but the observer does not know what the child is getting). Twenty of the twenty-two showed no change in behavior across the placebo and treatment conditions. Another group of researchers reviewed the evidence for the role of salicylates in foods and found it to be weak.

If Dr. Feingold's salicylate hypothesis were true, the incidence of ADD should have fallen, as has Reye's syndrome since the use of aspirin has been substantially decreased due to its association with that disease. In today's America, where fifty percent of mothers work, Dr. Feingold's diet would drive mothers from work and restrict their children from school lunch, birthday parties, barbecues, and eat-outs.

However, Dr. Feingold did make an important contribution by establishing that symptoms such as inattention and hyperactivity can be caused in a few children by allergic or nonallergic sensitivity to a particular food or food additive. A food additive is defined as a substance—or a mixture of substances—which is not a basic foodstuff, but is present in the food as a result of production, processing, storage, or packaging of the food. Food additives include preservatives, nutrients, flavoring agents, coloring agents, and texturizing agents.

A well-done study, performed on twenty-six children with ADD, however, does suggest some benefit from elimination diet in children with ADD, especially those with allergic diathesis. All nineteen children who benefited reacted to many foods, dyes, and/or preservatives. However, I do not agree with the author's conclusion that "dietary factors may play a significant role in the etiology of the majority of children with ADHD"—results that cannot be generalized to the vast majority of children with ADD who are not sensitive to foods, preservatives and artificial colorings, or do not have allergic tendencies. About five percent of children with ADD may be sensitive to food additives or other food items. In a Danish study, about one-to-two percent of school children were estimated to be intolerant of food colorings, flavors, and other additives, and most of those who reacted to food challenge had intestinal and skin symptoms besides behavioral symptoms. Parents of children with ADD should, therefore, observe whether eating particular foods makes the symptoms of their children worse; and physicians should take a history of allergies, especially food allergies, in the work-up of a patient with ADD. If a parent observes that a child's behavior improves on the elimination of a particular food, that food should be eliminated from the child's diet. However, do not deprive all children with ADD of culinary pleasures without proof of a food allergy. Such a practice is unreasonable and too restrictive. It can cause in psychological problems in the child.

Although it is popularly believed that medications for asthma cause hyperactivity, two population-based studies failed to show any relation between asthma and behavior. The response to a few-food diet—also called an oligoantigenic diet—has been studied by a group of researchers and has not been found to be meaningful clinically.

Others—such as, Dr. Doris Rapp (author of *Allergies and Your Family* and *Is This Your Child? Discovering and Treating Unrecognized Allergies*) and Dr. Mary Block (author of *No More Ritalin: Treating ADHD without Drugs*)—extended the Feingold hypothesis to include all kinds of allergies as the cause of ADD. Both authors support their cause with rhetoric rather than reason. Many good reviews of dietary therapies have returned the verdict of "not-useful in ADD" for elimination diets.

The issue of food and behavior has become highly politicized in the United States. Despite policy statements by the National Institute of Mental Health and the Food and Drug Administration about the limited role of food in causing abnormal behaviors in children, special interest groups—such as the Center for Science in Public Interest (CPSI)—keep the debate alive. CPSI has issued a report, *Diet, ADHD and Behavior,* and a brochure, *A Parent's Guide to Diet, ADHD and Behavior,* citing only those studies that show a relation between food and ADD, and ignoring those that do not. Journalists on the food-causes-ADD side of the debate also quote data that support their personal slant, omitting the larger body of data that does not support a relation between food and behavior.

I suggest that parents of children with ADD observe their children for signs of allergies—such as, hay fever, asthma, or allergic conjunctivitis. If a child has such symptoms, parents should get his allergies treated before trying psychostimulants. But if your child does not have the classic signs of allergy, do not keep looking for allergic zebras in the woods. By the time you come out of the woods, you will have lost your mind as well as your wallet. Allergy treatments are neither cheap nor harmless.

24

Do Children Outgrow ADD?

Except for an occasional child who learns to inhibit him or herself as he or she grows older, most individuals with ADD continue to manifest a few symptoms of ADD throughout life, albeit in a diminished or altered form. Inattentiveness persists throughout life. Although hyperactivity and intrusiveness decrease due to social inhibition, about fifty-to-sixty percent of children continue to show impulsivity and fidgetiness as adults. Do you recall a person sitting in the theater next to you, turning in his seat, changing hands on the armrest, and talking to himself? Such a person's impulsivity results in risky trades on the stock market, accidents, and frequent job changes. Although he may not be distracted by external stimuli—such as the opening of a door or the passing of a car—as he was as a child, his mind wanders from the Himalayas to Timbuktu when he is supposedly working in his office, trying to solve a problem.

Fewer children with ADD graduate from high school or finish college. The income and occupational achievement of these children is less than those of the general population from similar backgrounds. Poor management of ADD in childhood often results in juvenile delinquency and substance abuse. Children with ADD become adults showing higher rates of antisocial behavior, drug abuse, and mental illness.

Adolescence is a very challenging time for children with ADD. Many of them are apprehensive about college and are anxious about the loss of support they have been getting at home and at school. Many feel that they are different from other kids and become depressed. The outcome of the adolescent turmoil depends on self-acceptance, self-denial, or identity confusion. Children who are accepting of their differences are more likely to adapt to them, those in prolonged denial are more likely to rebel and get into trouble, and the confused are likely to take longer to assume adult roles.

Associating with the right kind of peers is a very important factor that determines the ultimate outcome of children with ADD. According to Judith Rich

Harris, author of *The Nurture Assumption,* peers have a seminal influence on children, much stronger than the influence of parents. However, the chicken-and-egg issue is not yet decided in this parent versus peers debate. Do peers shape the behavior of children or do the children gravitate toward their kind of peers, overachievers associating with overachievers and underachievers associating with underachievers? Although parents have very little influence over the kind of friends their children "hang out" with, they should be watchful of children who indulge in antisocial activities or are members of gangs. Parents should keep their children away from such extreme elements, even if it involves relocating.

Rejection by peers in the early elementary grades is one of the strongest predictors of poor outcome in ADD. I worry about a child who does not have friends and constantly complains that others are mean to him, especially if it happens in the classroom, in the neighborhood, and in the summer camp. Again it is not clear if children are rejected by peers because they have more severe problems, or if those who are rejected develop more severe problems due to rejection.

Some children who are hyperactive and disinhibited in elementary school develop the ability to sustain attention and control their impulsivity as they as grow older. The neurological processes that underlie attention and disinhibition follow a developmental course as does a child's ability to walk and talk. Such children appear to outgrow ADD, but, perhaps, they never had a disorder of attention, only developmental delay in the attentional domain.

"Whether something is good or bad depends upon the way you see it."

ROBERT AND JANE HANDLY,
*The Life*plus Program for Getting Unstuck*

25

Is Everything Lost in ADD?

ADD can be considered a byproduct of human evolution. Impulsivity and distractibility were advantageous to the primitive hunter-gatherer man because they saved him from predators. As man settled in safe colonies, he was no longer required to be aware of environmental distractions all the time. He learned to shut out unnecessary distractions from conscious awareness so that he could think and plan. The traits of distractibilty and impulsivity became undesirable in the new society. However, there are situations in which the wide panorama of the ADD mind and its quick responses, can still be harnessed productively. Swimming, horseback riding, and soccer are some of the activities in which children with ADD can succeed. Martial arts can help them rein in their energy.

The aphorism that the cup is half full and half empty is nowhere more true than in ADD. Children and adults with ADD have many positive traits, such as divergent thinking, the ability to think about and do many things at the same time, imagination and creativity, and liveliness and energy. With proper support and structure, the child may succeed in many activities, and, if focused and channeled, this energy can be harnessed to achieve.

There are many professions that require relatively short bytes of attention and high levels of energy and creativity—for example, a disc jockey, aerobic fitness instructor, nursery school teacher, and recreation therapist. According to author and special education expert Thomas Armstrong, activating "positive career aspirations" is a useful therapeutic tool for children with ADD. Parents and teachers should look beyond the boring world of the 3R's to find a suitable vocation for their children with ADD. Finding a skill or activity in which the child does well and building the child's self esteem that activity is an important part of managing children with ADD. I had a child in my practice who used to disrupt his class by doing all kinds of acrobatics, somersaults, and flips. His mother enrolled him in the Big Apple Circus. He did so well that he was featured in *The New York Times*. With pride, he brought the clipping for me to display in my office. A girl with ADD struggled throughout her school years, but found a niche in the day care business. Taking care of tiny tots does not require too much sustained attention, and she excels and revels in taking care of young children.

Diagnostic labels sometimes have bad connotations for the present and foreboding for the future. They tend to ignore that most diseases occur along a wide spectrum, with both weaknesses and strengths. We should work on the strengths of children with ADD, maintaining cautious optimism for the future, instead of stigmatizing them for their weaknesses, dooming their present and future.

With all these advances in pharmacology, based on our increasing understanding of biological functions, there is a parallel shift back to the Middle Ages in the form of an irrational faith in therapies with no scientific validity. Warning signs are the increase in sales of homoeopathic and herbal remedies, and the demand for 'pranotherapy' or other exotic and unproven medical practices."

SILVIO GARATTINI,
"'Pharmacocentricity': From Elixirs to Magic Bullets," LANCET

26

What About Alternative Treatments for ADD?

Alternative and complementary treatments are treatments that are not commonly used, or accepted, by practitioners of conventional medicine. Alternative and complementary treatments for ADD are flying high on the wings of anti-Ritalin propaganda by Christian Science and other groups. Even a few practitioners of conventional medicine are jumping on the bandwagon of alternative medicine. I am describing these treatments, not because I endorse or condone them, but because they are a New Age fad and because the consumer should be aware of their pros and cons. These treatments have been classified into seven categories by the National Center for Complementary and Alternative Medicine (NCCAM) of the National Institutes of Health, in Bethesda, Maryland.

Mind/body medicine: Mind/body medicine involves behavioral, psychological, social, and spiritual attempts to treat the body by exerting the influence of the mind over the body. The mind is the sum total of our thoughts, feelings, and memories. Each of our thoughts, feelings, and memories is a chemical or electrical wave in the brain that has the potential of circulating through the entire body. Thus, mind and body are intricately interlinked and constantly affect each other.

Treatments are rarely delivered alone; instead, they are used in combination with lifestyle interventions or are part of a traditional medical system. Yoga, biofeedback, and hypnosis are three treatments that have been suggested for ADD.

Yoga: Yoga postures, if performed with the correct breathing, are alleged to promote quietness and serenity of mind. Although yoga is a Hindu religious practice, the postures do not have any religious connotation and have become popular in the West. Children as young as six years can be taught yoga postures. Because yoga as a treatment modality for ADD has not been studied, I will not argue for or against it. Exercise is good for the body anyway, and it enhances a child's self-control and feeling of self-mastery. I do not see any reason why parents cannot try it as long as they understand that it does not have miraculous healing powers and should be used in conjunction with conventional treatments for ADD.

Like yoga, karate is claimed to decrease the symptoms of ADD. According to karate instructors, karate teaches concentration, self-control, self-discipline, and the ability to think before one acts—skills that children with ADD typically lack.

EEG biofeedback: EEG biofeedback involves applying electrodes to the child's head. The electrodes send electrical signals to a computer that gives a visual (lighting of a lamp or a specific pattern on the video screen) or an audible (a beep) signal to the child when there is an excess of theta waves in the frontal lobes of the brain. The child then tries to consciously increase beta waves and decrease theta waves by maintaining behavior associated with beta waves. Beta waves are fast waves associated with brain activity; theta waves are slow wave associated with brain inactivity.

Biofeedback is time-intensive (one or two sessions per week up to thirty to fifty sessions) and costly ($3,000 to $6,000). Most medical insurance organizations (MCO's) do not cover it. Its effects last only as long as it is provided; and, therefore, it is like suppressing a fever with tepid sponging rather than treating the cause of the fever. Biofeedback should not be used if the child has a history of seizures, depression, or hallucinations.

Dr. Joel F. Lubar and colleagues at the Southwestern Biofeedback Institute have reported that EEG biofeedback improves the behavior of children with ADD, but the studies had small samples and were open—that is, the experimenter knew what treatment a child was getting, thus introducing observer bias. Additionally, because the treatment was prolonged, the children involved may have matured with age. Dr. S.W. Lee and colleagues reviewed thirty-six studies in which biofeedback was used as a treatment for hyperactivity. They concluded that biofeedback treatments alone have not been effectively evaluated and that the results of present studies cannot be generalized to hyperactive populations because of methodological problems with them.

Behavioral relaxation training and other treatments: Other treatments that have been mentioned in the context of ADD include behavioral relaxation training (BRT), hypnosis, meditation, imagery, Christian Science spiritual healing, and art, music, and dance therapy. Both individual and group relaxation training (BRT) have been claimed to be effective in producing relaxed behavior and reduction of parent-reported symptoms of hyperactivity. Relaxation can be induced by an instructor through suggestions and hypnosis or it can be self-induced by self-suggestions and imagery. Feedback from the forehead muscle—called the Frontalis muscle—has also been used to teach relaxation. Like EEG biofeedback, these treatments are prolonged and costly, and their effects last only as long they are provided. There is no evidence that these treatments cure ADD, but they can certainly help in coping with it.

Biologically based therapies: This category includes natural and biologically based practices, interventions, and products, including the following: phytotherapy, or herbalism; special diet therapies; orthomolecular medicine; and unconventional pharmacological, biological, and instrumental interventions.

These treatments have become popular on the heels of the notoriety that industrial chemicals earned in the twentieth century as environmental pollutants. The discovery of chromosomal defects among children born in the Love Canal neighborhood of Niagara Falls, due to the dumping of industrial waste by Hooker Chemicals and Plastics Corporation, set in motion a number of epidemiological and scientific inquiries into the role of chemicals in everything from autism to breast cancer. Media hype through novels, movies (*A Civil Action*), and television shows has etched the diabolical nature of chemicals on the public psyche. The public, generalizing the evil influence of a few chemicals to all chemicals, is yearning to go green and organic. It is this yearning for natural remedies that underlies the recent upsurge of biological treatments for ADD. Patients passionately appeal to physicians not to prescribe Ritalin: "Doc, I do not want my child to get another chemical. Can't you try something natural?" In fact, deferring to the wishes of parents, I, too, have tried valerian, chamomile, ginkgo biloba, and St. John's Wort in some cases. In almost all the cases, I had to ultimately resort to Ritalin after one or two lost semesters of academic failure at school and tension at home.

The following are some of biologically-based therapies currently being used for ADD.

Pycnogenel: Obtained from the bark of a pine tree grown in Europe, pycnogenel contains phytochemicals called proanthrocyanidins, which are powerful antioxidants. While some therapeutic effects of pycnogenel have been documented in degenerative disorders such as aging-related cataracts, there are no controlled trials to prove that pycnogenel is beneficial in ADD, and there are no biologically plausible explanations about its possible role in ADD. There is no evidence that ADD is caused by wear and tear where antioxidants could be of help. Pycnogenel is costly and has to be taken in a very high dose initially to saturate the body with antioxidants. The sponsors of this herb caution the consumers against using adulterated and less potent products, indirectly urging them to buy the sponsors' brands.

Grapeseed extract: This is a cheaper alternative for pycnogenel, containing the same chemicals—proanthrocyanidins—as pycnogenel. Again, no clinical trials are available to establish that it can cure or ameliorate ADD.

Pycnogenel and grape seed extract are not reimbursed by MCO's and pycnogenel, at least, is not cheap. I am not aware of any report of serious side effects of either of these two herbs. In other words, these therapies have a low risk/benefit ratio, and, therefore, I do not argue against their use if the parents want to try these before resorting to Ritalin.

Super Blue Green™ algae: These algae grow in the waters of Upper Klamath Lake, located in southern Oregon. Sold as a nutritional supplement uncontaminated by chemicals, these algae are supposed to contain antioxidants, vitamins, minerals, and trace metals. There is no evidence that ADD is caused by nutritional deficiency. If this were so, ADD would be more common in the poorer countries of the world than in the United States, which is not the case. Once again, if parents want to try this product, I do not dissuade them lest I sound too paternalistic and dogmatic. The ability to choose their own treatments gives them autonomy, a feeling that is worth more than the little dent in their pocketbook.

Ginkgo biloba: The standardized extract of gingko—called EGb 761—is made from the leaves of the plant Ginkgo biloba and contains twenty-four percent flavone glycosides and six percent terpenelactones. One well-done study showed that this substance slows the progress of Alzheimer's disease by increasing blood flow to the brain. Gingko is also touted as an antioxidant that prevents damage by free radicals. It also affects neurotransmitter function in the brain. However, the herbal medicine camp is—without proof—extrapolating this finding to other conditions, such as ADD. Although a few side effects—such as headache, stomach upset, and allergic skin reaction—are known to occur, this substance is considered safe by regulatory agencies outside of the United States—such as German Commission E, a leading agency in the world for the regulation of herbs. Ginkgo should not be given with aspirin, because it can enhance the blood-thinning action of aspirin and induce bleeding. Because of its relative safety and low cost, I do not argue one way or the other if someone wants to try it.

St. John's Wort (Hypericum perforatum): A few clinical trials have shown that this herb ameliorates moderate depression. Its effects are mediated by two substances called hypericin and pseudohypericin. As with all herbs, the preparations in the market vary widely in the content of the active ingredients. The use of St John's Wort in ADD is not supported by studies and is an extrapolation. However, if a child with ADD is depressed, this treatment may be tried. Drug interactions with other medications used to treat ADD are not known.

Chamomile: Popular among some ethnic groups for the treatment of infantile colic and "nerves", chamomile can be given in the form of an extract or tea. It may act as a weak sedative, but is not specific for ADD. It is reasonably safe and is approved by the German Commission E.

However, these are no research studies that support its use in ADD.

Detoxifying teas—such as red clover, lemongrass and milk thistle—have also been recommended for ADD, without any evidence for or against them.

Valerian: Valerian root is a general sedative that is used in many commercial preparations for inducing sleep, such as Nite-Nite. ADD is not a sleep disorder; therefore, it is not rational to use valerian for treating it. On the other hand, if a child with ADD has difficulty in falling asleep, valerian may be helpful. No side effects have been reported.

Evening primrose oil (essential fatty acids): Although low levels of essential fatty acids (EFAs) have been observed in children with ADD by two independent group of researchers, it is not clear if these low levels were responsible for the abnormal behaviors of ADD patients or were a coincidence. EFAs, such as gamma-linolenic acid, are polyunsaturated fatty acids that serve as the building blocks for an important class of chemicals in the body, called prostaglandins. A double-blind trial of Efamol in eighteen boys with ADD, ages six to twelve years, was inconclusive. Only the Hyperactivity Factor on the teachers' rating scale showed a significant trend of Efamol effect between placebo and D-amphetamine, whereas the parents' ratings were not changed. Efamol contains evening primrose oil with vitamin E as a preservative. Similarly, EFA supplementation was noted to produce minimal or no improvements in hyperactive children selected without regard to baseline EFA concentrations. EFA supplementation resulted in a significant effect in only two of forty-two variables in thirty-one children with marked inattention and overactivity in a double-blind, placebo-controlled crossover study.

Although the evidence for the efficacy of EFAs in children with ADD is weak, EFAs are neither harmful nor costly; therefore, if you want to try them before trying Ritalin or other medications, feel free to do so.

5-Hydroxytryptophan (5-HTP): Tryptophan is an essential amino acid found in milk, cheeses, soybeans, meat, eggs, and nuts. It is required for the formation of serotonin, a neurotransmitter that is believed to be involved in emotional regulation. Although 5-hydroxytryptophan (5-HTP) is prescribed by naturopaths to treat a number of disorders—such as depression, ADD, migraine, and eating disorder—by supposedly restoring low levels of serotonin in the brain to normality, there is no scientific evidence that 5-HTP is actually converted to serotonin in significant quantities. In fact, its use and the use of its cousin, L-tryptophan, is associated with a condition called eosinophilic myalgia (EMS), a serious disease characterized by fever, weakness, shortness of breath, and high counts of a type of blood cell called eosinophil. L-tryptophan was removed by the FDA from shelves in 1989 after fifty people were reported to have died from EMS caused by it. Proponents of 5-HTP claim that this fatal reaction was caused by a contaminant, called peak x, in one of the brands, and not by 5-HTP. Presently, 5-HTP is being investigated by the FDA for its toxic effects.

L-tyrosine: The makers of a nutritional product called Focus claim that by increasing the intake of L-tyrosine through diet or supplements it is possible to increase the amount of dopamine and norepinephrine available in the brain. L-tyrosine is an amino acid (a protein) that the body uses to synthesize dopamine and norepinephrine, the two neurotransmitters believed to be involved in ADD. The idea of administering the building blocks for a complex chemical, with the hope of increasing the levels of that chemical in the body, appears intuitively very appealing, but the road from the raw precursors to the substance is often long and full of road blocks. The precursors have to be digested, and than have to reach the cellular factories in the brain which is insulated from the rest of the body by a chemical Berlin Wall called the blood-brain barrier. The formation of neurotransmitters is not determined solely by the availability of the precursors, but by the individual needs of the nerve cells at that point of time. The production is not limited by precursors but by a complex system of checks and balances. Neither the deficiency of L-tyrosine, nor the benefits of supplying it from outside, have been confirmed in scientific studies.

Deanol (DMAE), a precursor of acetylcholine, a neurotransmitter in the brain, is also cited as being beneficial. More research is needed before precursors can be recommended for ADD.

Calmplex-2000: This is a homeopathic remedy containing gluconic DMG (N,N-Dimethylglycine). Like other alternative treatments, it is also recommended for a wide variety of conditions, such as autism and ADD. Homeopathic remedies are used in very small doses and are believed to work on the principle of similia similibus curantor, that is, "like treats like."

For example, a very dilute solution of lead is likely to cure lead poisoning. The homeopaths give a pseudoscientific argument that a small dose of a toxic substance acts as a hapten—or allergen—stimulating the formation of antibodies, but they do not subscribe to the general principles of allergy to prove their point. The more dilute a substance is, the more potent it is believed to be. Despite the small dose, side effects called aggravations can sometimes occur. There are no case-control studies that have evaluated homeopathic treatment of ADD.

Anti-motion sickness medicines: These medicines are prescribed by some practitioners in the belief that ADD occurs due to defects of the vestibular system, a part of the inner ear that helps in maintaining balance. The brain gets confused by the incoming sensations, resulting in "sensory scrambling," and anti-motion sickness medicines—such as Dramamine—help cure the deficit. There is no scientific evidence for this theory, and if disturbance of the vestibular system were to cause ADD, children with ADD would not be able to ride on roller coasters or Ferris wheels. On the contrary, children with ADD love the titillation of such scream machines.

Inositol: According to a controlled trial listed in the Cochrane Library Index of clinical trials, inositol has been found to worsen the symptoms of ADD.

Magnesium and zinc: In one study, magnesium deficiency was reported in a few patients of ADD, and magnesium supplementation at the dose of 200-mg/day actually improved the symptoms of ADD. Magnesium might have acted as a general sedative in this study, and the finding of magnesium deficiency and benefits of magnesium has not been confirmed by any other study. Zinc deficiency has also been incriminated as a cause of ADD. As long as a recommended dietary dose of zinc is taken daily, it is not a problem; but excessive doses of zinc are harmful for the nervous system.

Megavitamins (orthomolecular therapy): High doses—ten to twelve times the daily recommended dietary allowance (RDA)—of two vitamins of the B-complex—niacinamide (B1) and pyridoxine (B6)—have been claimed to be useful in autism and ADD. However, a well-done study showed that there was no difference in the behavior of children who received high doses of ascorbic acid (vitamin C) and three members of the B-complex family of vitamins: niacinamide, calcium pantothenate, and pyridoxine, and those children who did not. Blood levels of the vitamins in the two groups were similar. As many as forty-two percent of the children who received megadoses of vitamins had elevated levels of liver enzymes, suggesting liver damage. Children exhibited twenty-five percent more disruptive classroom behavior when treated with vitamins versus a placebo.

Pirecetam: This substance belongs to a class of drugs called the nootropics, substances that enhance intelligence. It has been found to be beneficial in dementia and dyslexia, but its effect on the symptoms of ADD has not been studied. There is some theoretical basis for its efficacy in ADD, because it increases dopamine neurotransmission in the brain. Therefore, I will not argue against its use in a child who has both dyslexia and ADD, but will try conventional medications, such as methylphenidate, for uncomplicated ADD. At present, pirecetam is not available in the United States.

Anti-yeast therapy: Candida albicans, a yeast, is normally found in various parts of the body, including the gut. Generally, the amount of yeast in the gut is kept under control by other microbes that compete for the same nourishment. However, exposure to antibiotics—especially repeated exposure—can destroy these microbes, resulting in an overgrowth of candida albicans. According to the proponents of the yeast theory of ADD and autism (William Crook, in *The Yeast Connection*), when the yeast multiplies, it releases toxins—such as aldehyde, alcohol, tartaric acid, and other organic acids—which, in turn, impair the central nervous system and the immune system. Only one lab in the country, owned by a proponent of the candida theory, tests the urine for the toxic metabolites of candida. The promoters of this theory recommend that this test—costing about $200— be done at the initiation of therapy and then periodically thereafter. No other commercial lab tests for these substances; medical insurers do not reimburse the cost.

Some of the behavioral problems that have been linked to an overgrowth of candida albicans include confusion, hyperactivity, short attention span, lethargy, irritability, and aggression. Health problems—such as headaches, stomachaches, constipation, gas pains, fatigue, and depression—have also been attributed to candida.

Treatment is begun with an antifungal antibiotic: nystatin. If this does not work, other antifungal antibiotics—amphotericin B and ketoconazole (Nizoral)—are tried. Whereas nystatin is safe, the other two are not so benign and may cause side effects. All are given orally. Additionally, the gut is replenished with the "good" microbes (e.g., acidophilus) by giving a rich culture of these microbes to the child. Overgrowth of the yeast is prevented by avoiding sugar and other foods on which yeast thrives.

Interestingly, the child is supposed to become ill and to show negative behaviors for a few days after receiving antifungal treatment, because the yeast is destroyed and the debris is circulated through the body until it is excreted. A child who shows such deterioration is believed to have a good prognosis.

All evidence is anecdotal, written up in well-marketed books. There is no evidence that there is overgrowth of candida in individuals with ADD. If overgrowth of candida were to cause ADD, many women with vaginal candidiasis and many men with HIV would become intensely hyperactive and inattentive. Candida causes an itch, not ADD.

The number of biological agents being promoted on the Internet as treatments of ADD is too great for me to elaborate. The first amendment of the United States Constitution allows the purveyors of snake oil freedom of expression, but consumers should use their freedom of thought—an innate faculty with which we are born—to assess the merits of any claim the charlatans make. Unfortunately, alternative medicine is the in thing right now, with an aura of a popular uprising against conventional medicine. Therefore, I am cautious about outrightly rejecting these treatments. If a treatment is not harmful, even if not useful, I do not dissuade parents from trying it. If a treatment is potentially harmful, I caution parents, but I am not paternalistic in forbidding its use. Parents should decide for themselves what is good for their child and their family. The physician can assist them in this process, but should not usurp their autonomy.

Manipulative and body-based systems: This category refers to systems that use manipulation and/or movement of the body—such as chiropractic medicine, massage and body work—and unconventional physical and occupational therapies.

Chiropractic: Chiropractors claim that most diseases are caused by misalignment of spinal and peripheral joints and, therefore, can be treated by chiropractic manipulation. It does not make scientific sense that the manipulation of certain joints can cure ADD, but some placebo effect on the ability to concentrate and focus can occur due to the personal attention the child receives from another adult who tells him to focus and stay still. Whereas chiropractic manipulation is valuable in diseases of bone and joints, according to Paul G. Shekelle of the Veterans Affairs Medical Center, Los Angeles, California, there is little evidence to support the use of chiropractic manipulation in other diseases. Chiropractors from two reputable chiropractic schools in Canada and the United States conducted a randomized, controlled trial of chiropractic spinal manipulation in mild to moderate asthma, but did not find any additional benefit of spinal manipulation over the standard medical management of asthma. In a well-done study published in the *Journal of the American Medical Association*, chiropractic manipulation was not found to be helpful in cases of tension headache.

Sensorimotor integration: The practitioners of sensorimotor integration postulate that ADD occurs because impulses from various sensory modalities—such as vision, hearing, and the vestibular system (the balancing system)—are not received by their brain in an organized and integrated manner. In other words, the brain is overwhelmed by incoming sensations. Just imagine a vocalist, a drummer, a juggler, and a vaudevillian all coming on the stage at the same time without any planning and coordination. According to Dr. A. Jean Ayres—author of *Sensory Integration and the Child* and the originator of this therapy—the vestibular system plays a key role in this integrative process. Sensorimotor integration involves strengthening the vestibular system so that the brain can integrate incoming sensations through the various senses.

There is no evidence that ADD is caused by sensorimotor disintegration and that occupational therapy has any role in its treatment. However, if parents feel that their child is sensitive to touch, light, or sound, they should have the child examined by a therapist who specializes in sensorimotor integration. And if a problem is confirmed, the child should be treated. But to subject all children with ADD to this treatment modality is a travesty of medicine.

Similarly, there is no evidence that changing visual perception with colored glasses and prisms and changing auditory perception with narrow band music can cure ADD. There is no scientific proof that auditory stimulation and listening training with high-frequency human voice and music—as recommended by Dr. Tomatis, a French otolaryngologist—can cure or control ADD.

Alternative medical systems: These include medical systems that have been practiced in other parts of the world since antiquity. Each of these systems has its unique explanation of how diseases are caused and how they should be treated.

Acupuncture: This is the traditional Chinese method of treating a number of diseases by injecting special needles at specific points in the body through which life energy flows—called Qi (pronounced chi) in Chinese. Practitioners specializing in children can persuade children to withstand the pain of needle insertion. At present, there is a dearth of properly trained and accredited professionals in acupuncture. It is a costly treatment and its benefits in ADD have not yet been confirmed. The National Institute of Mental Health has funded a study of laser acupuncture for treatment of ADD, at Santa Clara Valley Medical Center in San Jose, California, but the results are not out as yet.

Ayurveda: Ayurveda is the ancient Indian science of longevity. It postulates that there are three types of human constitution, called doshas. All diseases occur because of imbalance in kapha, pitta, and vata, the three doshas. Individuals with excess vata are restless and absent-minded. They are impatient, indecisive, and have short memory. Individuals with excess kapha, on the other hand, are calm, slow, tolerant, and forgiving. ADD occurs because of excess of vata and shortage of kapha. Practitioners of Ayurveda try to restore this imbalance by lifestyle changes, diet, yoga, breathing, and herbs.

Whereas the individual temperaments that Ayurveda describes are very similar to what has been discovered by modern psychologists and psychiatrists, the treatments that are offered are not standardized or validated. I may go along with lifestyle changes—yoga and breathing exercises—but would be wary of trying Ayurvedic herbs, body-cleansing enemas, and oil massage, without any proof of their safety and efficacy.

Lifestyle and Disease Prevention: This category involves practices designed to identify and treat risk factors, thereby preventing the development of illness. It includes health promotion, clinical preventative practices, clinical ecology, and lifestyle therapies. In the context of ADD, lifestyle management would involve improving the goodness of fit between the temperament of the child and the parenting style of the parents. Dietary changes—such as avoiding sugar and sweeteners to prevent hyperactivity, and avoiding distractions—would belong to this category. Thomas Armstrong has described "50 Ways to Improve Your Child's Behavior and Attention Span Without Drugs, Labels, or Coercion" in his book *The Myth of the ADD*. Peter Breggin, the author of *Toxic Psychiatry*, also argues for treating ADD with lifestyle changes alone. While their intentions are good, their diatribe against medications is unfounded. Lifestyle changes are helpful—actually essential—in coping with and caring for a child with ADD, but by themselves cannot cure ADD, just as dietary changes alone cannot cure diabetes, high blood pressure, or coronary heart disease, in most patients.

Biofield: Biofield medicine involves systems that use subtle energy fields in and around the body for medical purposes and includes therapeutic touch and natural healing. In India it is very common for the afflicted to touch the feet of a guru in the belief that the guru's energy would pass to them, healing them in this process. There is no evidence that therapeutic touch can cure ADD; however, it can have a placebo effect in the faithful. As long as the practitioners of therapeutic touch do not claim that it can cure ADD and do not ask for large sums of money, it seems to be a harmless practice.

Bioelectromagnetics: Bioelectromagnetics refers to the unconventional use of electromagnetic fields for medical purposes. I am not aware of any report that supports the use of bioelectromagnetic fields in ADD.

27

Is Alternative Medicine Fact or Fiction?
THE MYTH OF MIRACLES AND MAGIC

Man has always been fascinated by myth, miracles, and magic. He creates myth to explain what he does not know, miracles to rationalize what happens without his control, and magic to vicariously control what he rationally cannot. The cause and treatment of ADD are still mired in mystery; therefore, ADD is fertile ground for the purveyors of miracle and magic, the practitioners of irrational, euphemistically called "alternative," medicine. To sow the seeds of hope for the hopeless, they recommend herbs, dietary manipulation, detoxification, body-mind mumbo jumbo, and magical potions—and might even conjure up a genie who would say "abracadabra" to flick ADD away.

I do not want to take away hope from people disenchanted with mainstream medicine, but I want to temper it with reality by proposing the following scheme to judge the merits of treatments and the claims and veracity of the agents of the "journey of hope." My sole purpose is to provide information to parents so that they can avoid harm and loss.

Hearsay versus research: Check if a therapy is backed by credible scientific research performed by a number of researchers working independently. Word of mouth, multisyllabic words, a few testimonials, and sponsored programs that make tall claims for a product are not sufficient. Do not decide in favor of a treatment just because the *New York Times* or a radio talk show reports a sensational study about it. Although reporters, editors, and publishers may make every attempt to check the accuracy of their reports, they cannot achieve the rigor of science. Studies, like evidence presented in a court of law, should be cross-examined to see if they were published in a reputable journal, if they were conducted properly, and if the patients included in the study were similar to those who will be treated by the proposed therapy. Was the improvement in the group that received treatment significantly greater than the improvement in a comparison group of similar patients who did not receive the treatment?

Was the trial blinded, that is, neither the researcher nor the child knew if the child received the treatment under study or a dummy treatment—technically called *placebo*—until the final analysis? Blinding is essential to avoid observer bias. Eyes have a tendency to see what the mind wants to see and ignore what the mind does not want to see. Blinding prevents that bias. Purveyors of alternative medicine often quote poorly done studies and fault the scientific method of double-blind trials because they are too costly and are often sponsored by companies that have a financial interest in the medicine that is being tested. Double-blind trials are certainly rigorous, and rightfully so, because the health of millions of people worldwide depends on the proper evaluation of medicines before outlandish claims are made on their behalf. A few techniques, such as manipulation, are not amenable to a double-blind trial, but other statistical methods, such as single-subject designs, can be used to ascertain if a technique is useful or not.

It is a society's collective responsibility to oversee the health of its citizens; therefore, it is important to make a few ground rules to examine all therapeutic claims. Although individual experiences are important to generate new ideas and hypotheses, it is essential to compare a significantly large number of individuals who receive a treatment with those who do not (*paradigm of numbers* and *paradigm of comparison*), to see if the individual experience can be generalized to a large number of people. I prefer the framework of conventional science for examining therapeutic claims, although it should not be too rigorous as to stifle growth of new ideas.

Greed versus altruism: It is difficult for me to believe that the purveyors of snake oil promote their wares out of the goodness of their hearts for the benefit of ailing humanity. Everyone is in the business of making money. A month's supply of pycnogenel costs at least four times as much as a month's supply of Ritalin. A full course of biofeedback costs $3,000 to $6,000. The therapeutic love that some practitioners of alternative medicines provide may cost as much as $75 an hour.

Always try to find out if the provider of an alternative therapy has any financial interest in promoting a particular therapy. There is a potential conflict of interest if a study is funded by the maker of the drug; but, unfortunately, there is a Catch-22 here. Only a company that makes a new drug can supply it for a study. However, if the scientists performing a study are aboveboard and the scientists reviewing the study are men and women of integrity, this should not be a problem. One can check the National Health Fraud Unit, FDA, and the National Center for Complementary and Alternative Medicine (NCCAM) to find out if the claims of the alternative provider are extravagant and fraudulent.

Kidsplex story: Performance Nutrition, a Texas company that marketed a product called Kidsplex as a drug-free alternative to ADD medication, was sued because the company had misrepresented the lack of clinical support it had for this product as a treatment of ADD. A class action lawsuit was filed in US District Court in Texas in 1996 against this company by Weiss and Yourman, lawyers for the plaintiffs. The suit alleged that the company and two former executives misrepresented and/or omitted material information about the company's business, outlook, and a past embezzlement conviction against the company's former CEO.

Science versus pseudoscience: Is there a scientific basis for the recommended therapy? Many purveyors use pseudoscience to beguile consumers. For example, chiropractors postulate that learning disability and ADD are caused by misalignment of the sphenoid bone at the base of the skull and the temporal bone at the side of skull. This misalignment somehow affects the function of the underlying brain, and they can fix it by manipulating the bones into proper position. This is not consistent with skull anatomy, because skull bones are joined to each other within a few years of birth and cannot be moved by manipulation. Moreover, the function of brain cells is not affected by the position of the overlying bones.

So far, alternative medicine has not fared well in scientific testing. Of the thirty research grants funded by the Office of Alternative Medicine of the National Institute of Medicine, only nine have resulted in published papers, five in journals not included in the National Library of Medicine catalog.

Risk versus benefit: Alternative and complementary treatments can be harmful, too. Providers of alternative therapy often claim that their treatments are free of side effects, whereas conventional medicines have many side effects and adverse effects. In her book, *God's Perfect Child*, Caroline Fraser narrates the tales of many Christian Science children who died due to the faith-healing practices of Christian Science-founder Mary Baker Eddy and her followers.

Many herbalists lure consumers by saying that herbs are not chemicals and are, therefore, not as harmful as the chemicals prescribed by purveyors of common medicine. Nothing could be farther from truth. More disease, death, and devastation in this world have been caused by two plant products—tobacco and cocoa—then all synthetic chemicals combined. Marijuana is a plant product, and so is opium. Another chemical—ephedrine—from the leaves of a plant grown in northern Africa, has hit the drug-abuse market as herbal ecstasy. The entire human body is a soup of hormones and neurotransmitters—which are chemicals.

Second, herbs also affect the body through organic chemicals they contain called phytochemicals, which also have the potential to be harmful. A few argue that herbal chemicals are not harmful because they are made by Mother Nature, but medicines are harmful because they are artificially synthesized in the laboratory. But salt is salt, whether it is obtained from the sea or made in the lab. In fact, a substance made in the lab is likely to be purer than one found in nature.

Herbal preparations are often not made under standardized conditions and their ingredients may vary from one batch to another. In a study, conducted by the California Department of Health Sciences, of the 260 Asian medicines marketed in the United States, 83 were found to contain undeclared pharmaceuticals or heavy metals, and 23 had more than one adulterant. Herbs containing anticholinergics are responsible for a number of deaths in developing countries each year. A 1998 issue of the *New England Journal of Medicine* (September 17) reports a number of cases showing the adverse effects of herbal medicines and dietary supplements.

Herbs can interact with other herbs and medicines, causing harmful drug interactions. For example, garlic can interact with coumadin (a drug given after stroke to decrease blood clotting) to cause bleeding. Herbs can result in allergic as well as idiosyncratic reactions in some individuals. Chaparral, an herb used to treat menopausal syndrome, resulted in a few cases of fatal liver disease and was withdrawn from the market. St. John's Wort makes the skin prone to sunburn.

Dietary supplements and megavitamins are also not without risk. Excessive doses of vitamin A and D can increase intracranial pressure. High doses of vitamin B6 and magnesium were associated with peripheral neuropathy in one study.

The 5-hydroxytryptophan (5-HTP) disaster: *In the aftermath of the passage of The Dietary Supplement Health and Education Act of 1994 (DSHEA) by the 103rd Congress, a nutritional supplement called 5-HTP* *was sold to overcome depression, insomnia, and obesity. Following its use, an epidemic of a deadly condition called eosinophilic myalgia (characterized by fever, muscle pains, weakness, and high white cell counts) occurred, with 50 fatalities. DSHEA permitted herbs, phytochemicals, and other chemicals to be sold as dietary supplements without FDA approval, provided that health or therapeutic claims were not specified on their labels. The FDA was charged with the burden of proving them unsafe before restricting their use.*

Medicine is not a matter of soundbites or hucksterism. Look at the fundamentals of any tall claim. If it is an herb, check the Web pages of the Federal Drug Adminstration (FDA)—www.fda.gov—and of the Southwest School of Botanical Medicine—www.ard.grin—for its efficacy and toxicity. Find out how the herb should be used: as a tincture (alcoholic extract), as a tea, or in some other form. When was the preparation made and how was it stored? Unfortunately, there are no standards for herbs in the United States. Herbalists often make outrageous claims and generalize the benefits of an herb from one disease to another without any proof. According to a popular self-help book of nutritional healing, an herb by the name of yellow dock reportedly acts as "a blood purifier and cleanser, tones the entire system, improves colon and liver function, is good for anemia, liver diseases, and skin disorders, such as, eczema, hives, psoriasis, and rashes." How is it good for anemia? What kind of anemia is it good for? How does it improve colon function, in diarrhea or in constipation? What kind of rashes is it good for? Do not depend entirely on the food store clerk for information, but ask your doctor about the herb you are thinking of trying. For other treatments,

check the Web site of the National Center for Complementary and Alternative Medicine (NCCAM)—http://nccam.nih.gov. *Alternative Medicine Alert,* a monthly newsletter published by the American Health Consultants, is also a good source of useful information about alternative treatments. The Federal Trade Commission is distributing a free consumer alert about fraudulent health advertising on the Internet, called *Virtual 'Treatments' Can Be Real-World Deceptions.* It can be obtained by writing to the Federal Trade Commission, Consumer Response Center, 600 Pennsylvania Ave., NW, Washington, DC 20580, or by calling 877-FTC-HELP (or 877-382-4357). Do not be afraid—and remember: *Caveat emptor!*

Use of alternative medicine can delay identification of the true problem, sometimes with fatal consequences. The newsletter of the National Council Against Health Fraud described the case of a seventeen-year-old whose Hodgkin's disease (a tumor of the lymph glands) progressed, dropping her chances of survival from 85 percent to 50 percent, because of the delay caused by administering alternative treatments instead of chemotherapy. My father, a great lover of Ayurveda, the ancient Indian science of longevity, was treated for bronchial asthma for many years by a practitioner of Ayurveda when he, in fact, had cardiac asthma. The treatment of the two conditions is diagonally opposite. A practitioner of homeopathy kept treating a patient for hemorrhoids, when the patient was actually bleeding due to colon cancer.

Popular? So what?: The increasing popularity of alternative or complementary medicine is often advanced as an argument for its validity and efficacy. Popularity is a political and show-biz concept, not a scientific concept. Alternative medicine is popular because it empowers the patient by engaging him in the therapeutic process as a decision maker rather than alienating him through paternalism. It is popular because it addresses the patient directly in his or her language rather than shrouding itself in some esoteric jargon; because it offers choices rather than deterministic finality to the patient; because it addresses the person who has the pathology, and not the pathological process only. And last but not least, it is popular because it is a fad. To argue that it must be effective because it is popular is like saying that violence must be right because it is so rampant. Science is not based upon Gallup polls. It is judged by validity, not by popularity. In a letter to the *New York Times*, Caroline Fraser, author of *God's Perfect Child*, said, "Thousands of people believe in all manner of things, testifying to abduction by space aliens and seeing Jesus in oil stains and tortillas; however sincere the believers and however large their numbers, their belief is not evidence of accuracy."

Qualified practitioners versus quacks: Practitioners of alternative medicine are often charismatic orators, well versed in the scientific and the new body-mind and holistic medicine jargon. In his book *American Health Quackery*, James Harvey Young quotes Arthur William Meyer describing a quack: "Bravado, self-adulation, a ready wit, and a double tongue, shrewdness, a knowledge of the foibles of men, a blunted conscience and an ignorance of the very things in which they claimed competence always have characterized the quack." The dictionary defines a quack as "a pretender to medical knowledge or skill;

ignorantly or falsely pretending to cure." The term quack is derived from quacksalver, or one who quacks like a duck in promoting his salves. Many are poorly qualified to practice the trade of healing. There are no standards for training, no accreditation, no licensing, and no regulatory oversight. The practitioners of alternative medicine "often oversell the promise of their treatments or assume too much baggage from the cornucopia of vague New Age culture." Just as you would not buy a stock based solely upon a promotion, do not buy an alternative medicine on the basis of a promotion, a radio talk show, or a sponsored program on television. It is not difficult to acquire testimonials or to purchase time on television or radio.

Alternative medicine has not been subjected to the same scrutiny and media exposure as conventional medicine, and I wonder if it will be able to withstand the rigor of science. If it does, it should be integrated into mainstream medicine. But reverting to the mindset when malaria was popularly believed to be due to bad air and schizophrenia due to witchcraft, will be going backwards to an unenlightened age.

28

Epilogue

In this book, I have summarized a few facts for parents of children with ADD. The human body is so complex that its mysteries will not be completely known for many millennia—and, perhaps, may never be known. Our state of knowledge about ADD is still in its infancy; hence all the myth and mystery surrounding it. Although myth and mystery are good for fiction, I prefer to tread on the beaten path. The beaten path I am referring to is the path of conventional medicine, a medicine that is based on rational thinking and empirical observations, a medicine that makes stringent requirements of its practitioners, requirements of truth and integrity, a medicine that has eradicated formidable foes—such as poliomyelitis and smallpox—and reduced infant mortality to single digits in this century.

I do not have any regrets for using methylphenidate (Ritalin) or other medications for many of my patients with ADD, because they work and work well if used judiciously. The use of Ritalin is grounded in body/mind medicine, because it restores the chemical imbalance in the brain—the seat of the mind—healing it in the process. The body follows suit, obeying the dictates of the mind. Ritalin is only as toxic as Tylenol—or the chemicals in Coca Cola or in grapeseed extract. It is not *Toxic Psychiatry* or *War Against Children*, as Peter Breggin, author of *Toxic Psychiatry,* argues. Love and psychotherapy alone cannot cure ADD, as many well-done studies testify. Even critics of Ritalin, such as Lawrence Diller, author of *Running on Ritalin,* end up using Ritalin for some of their patients—"sometimes I end up medicating children mainly because they cause problems for their parents or teachers, and the child benefits more indirectly"— contradicting their own thesis. However, Ritalin is only one of the pieces of the ADD puzzle. Completing the puzzle requires restoring the child's relations with his or her parents, siblings, and peers; his or her performance in the school; and his or her self-esteem. Call it holistic or whatever.

Whereas physical science has been splitting the atom into smaller and smaller particles, the trend in medicine in the 1990s was toward integration and "holism," treating the whole person rather than an organ or tissue of the body. Conventional medicine has become too mundane, too commonplace to be news for the media, which, therefore, has found a new sensation in body-mind, herbal, and holistic medicine. For the media, it is a strategic shift; for the modern gurus, it is a window of opportunity; and for the consumer, there is the hope that medicine will become "the common property of the people." So the purveyors of alternative medicine condemn conventional medicine in their bestsellers, on talk shows, and on the Internet, and try to gather their rosebuds while they may. Their agenda is not philanthropy or philosophy, but the chance to take a bite out of the healthcare pie. They cash in on the public disenchantment with the mechanical and mercenary-like attitude of the practitioners of conventional medicine. If the practitioners of conventional medicine become better communicators and share feelings—and not just facts—with their patients, we will not need charlatans and the sellers of snake oil.

It would be imprudent to discard alternative medicine lock, stock, and barrel, because alternative medicine has brought about a new consciousness about a healthy lifestyle, along with new techniques for relaxing and soothing the overworked minds and bodies of today. Alternative medicine has shifted the focus from pathology to person. Conventional and alternative medicine can be complementary instead of adversarial, if an eclectic approach to patient care is followed. If a child has an abnormal idiosyncratic reaction to sugar, a food additive, a dye, or a particular food, eliminate this substance from the diet; and if a child is overwhelmed by sounds, light, and touch, explore sensorimotor integration. If your child is stressed out, teach him relaxation through yoga or whichever technique works with him or her. But do not deprive your child of mainstream medicine just because you do not like it or you heard someone on television condemning it. Keep an open mind, consider all the options, and obtain the best of all worlds for you and your child.

Selected Bibliography

SECTION I

Is ADD Real or a Figment of the Imagination?

Accardo, Pasquale J. et al. *Attention Deficit Disorders and Hyperactivity in Children.* New York: Marcel Dekker, 1991.

American Psychiatric Association. *Diagnostic and Statistical Manual of Mental Disorders: DSM-IV.* 4th ed. Washington, DC: American Psychiatric Press, 1994.

Barkley, Russell A. *ADHD and the Nature of Self-Control.* New York: Guilford Publications, 1997.

Stowe, Harriett Beecher. *Uncle Tom's Cabin.* New York: HarperCollins Publications, 1987.

Why Is It Difficult to Accept ADD as a Disease?

Conners, C. Keith. *Conners' Rating Scales: Revised Technical Manual.* Tonawanda, NY: Multi-Health Systems, 1997.

Is ADD a New Disorder?

American Psychiatric Association. *Diagnostic and Statistical Manual of Mental Disorders: DSM-III.* 3rd ed. Washington, DC: American Psychiatric Press, 1980.

American Psychiatric Association. *Diagnostic and Statistical Manual of Mental Disorders: DSM-IV.* 4th ed. Washington, DC: American Psychiatric Press, 1994.

Barkley, Russell A. *ADHD and the Nature of Self-Control.* New York: Guilford Publications, 1997.

Hawthorne, Nathaniel. *Scarlet Letter.* New York: Bantam Books, 1981.

Hoffmann, Heinrich. *Struwwelpeter.* English Translation. Mineola, NY: Dover Publications, 1995.

Laufer, M., E. Denhoff, G. Solomons. "Hyperkinetic Impulse Disorder in Children's Behavior Problems." *Psychosomatic Medicine* 19 (1957): 38-49.

Still, G. F. "Some Abnormal Psychical Conditions in Children." *Lancet* 1 (1902): 1.

How Common Is ADD Anyway?

Anderson, D.R., S.R. Levin, E.P. Lorch. "The Effects of Television Program Pacing on the Behavior of Preschool Children." *AV Communication Review* 25 (1977): 154-166.

Anderson, D.R. and P.A. Collins. *The Impact on Children's Education: Television's Influence on Cognitive Development.* Washington, DC: US Department of Education, 1988.

Ehrenreich, B. "Think Quick: James Gleick's Fact-filled Book Examines the Rapidity of Modern Life." *New York Times Book Review*, September 12, 1999.

Gleick, James. *Faster: The Acceleration of Just About Everything.* New York: Pantheon Books, 1999.

Hoffman, R. *Natural Approach to Attention Deficit Disorder (ADD): Drug-Free Ways to Treat the Roots of This Childhood Epidemic.* New Canaan, CT: Keats Publishing, 1997.

Silver, Larry B. *Attention Deficit Disorder: A Clinical Guide to Diagnosis and Treatment.* Washington, DC: American Psychiatric Press, 1992.

Is ADD a Disease of the Affluent?

Glow, R. "How Common Is Hyperkinesis?" *Lancet* 1 (1980): 89.

Holborow, Patricia and Paul Berry. "A Multinational Multicultural Perspective on Hyperactivity." *American Journal of Orthopsychiatry* 56 (1986): 320-2.

Leung, Patrick W.L. et al. "The Diagnosis and Prevalence of Hyperactivity in Chinese Schoolboys." *British Journal of Psychiatry* 168 (1996): 486-96.

Rohde, L.A. et al. "ADHD in a School Sample of Brazilian Adolescents: A Study of Prevalence, Comorbid Conditions, and Impairments." *Journal of the American Academy of Child and Adolescent Psychiatry* 38 (1999): 716-22.

Taylor, E. and S. Sandberg. "Hyperactive Behavior in English Schoolchildren: A Questionnaire Survey." *Journal of Abnormal Child Psychology* 12 (1984): 143-56.

Does Bad Parenting Cause ADD?

Bolotin, S. "The Disciples of Discipline." *New York Times Magazine*, February 14, 1999.

Brenner, V. and R.A. Fox. "Parental Discipline and Behavior Problems in Young Children." *Journal of General Psychology* 159 (1998): 251-6.

Fraiberg, Selma H. *The Magic Years.* New York: Charles Scribner & Sons, 1959.

Harris, Judith Rich. *The Nurture Assumption: Why Children Turn Out the Way They Do: Parents Matter Less Than You Think and Peers Matter More.* New York: Simon & Schuster Trade, 1998.

————— "Where Is the Child's Environment? A Group Socialization Theory of Development." *Psychological Review* 102 (1995): 458-89.

Watt, Laura A. "Parents Blaming Parents." Letter to the Editor. *New York Times Magazine*, November 21, 1998.

Nix, R.L. et al. "The Relation Between Mothers' Hostile Attribution Tendencies and Children's Externalizing Behavior Problems: The Mediating Role of Mothers' Harsh Discipline Practices." *Child Development* 70 (1999): 896-909.

What Is Wrong with the ADD Brain?
Castellanos, F. Xavier. "Toward a Pathophysiology of Attention Deficit/Hyperactivity Disorder." *Clinical Pediatrics* 36 (1997): 381-404.

Malone, M.A., J. Kershner, J.M. Swanson. "Hemispheric Processing and Methylphenidate Effects in Attention-Deficit-Disorder." *Journal of Child Neurology* 9 (1994): 181-9.

Rosenberger, P.B. "Attention Deficit." *Pediatric Neurology* 7 (1991): 397-405.

Suffin, S.C. and W.H. Emory. *Neurometric Subgroups in Attentional and Affective Disorders and Their Association with Pharmacotherapeutic Outcome.* Thousand Oaks, CA: Ventura Institute of Psychiatry Medical Group, n.d.

Voeller, Kytja. "What Can Neurological Models of Attention, Inattention, and Arousal Tell Us About Attention-Deficit Hyperactivity Disorder?" *Journal of Neuropsychiatry* 3 (1991): 209-16.

What Causes ADD?
Shaywitz, Sally E. and Bennett A. Shaywitz. "Evaluation and Treatment of Children with Attention Deficit Disorders." *Pediatrics in Review* 6 (1984): 99-109.

Turecki, Stanley. *Normal Children Have Problems, Too: How Parents Can Understand and Help.* New York: Bantam Books, 1994.

Vernon, John. *A Book of Reasons.* New York: Houghton Mifflin Co., 1999.

Is ADD Only a Question of Difficult Temperament?
Carey, W. and S.C. McDevitt. *Clinical and Educational Applications of Temperament Research.* Amsterdam, The Netherlands: Swets & Zeitlinger, 1989.

Chess, Stella and Alexander Thomas. *Temperament in Clinical Practice.* New York: Guilford Publications, 1986.

Medoff-Cooper, B., W.B. Carey, S.C. McDevitt. "The Early Infancy Temperament Questionnaire." *Journal of Developmental Behavior Pediatrics* 14 (1993): 230-5.

Graziano, W.G., L.A. Jensen-Campbell, G.M. Sullivan-Logan. "Temperament, Activity, and Expectations for Later Personality Development." *Journal of Perspectives in Social Psychology* 74 (1998): 1266-77.

Can Parents Diagnose ADD by Using Questionnaires?

Hallowell, Edward. *When You Worry About the Child You Love: Emotional and Learning Problems in Children.* New York: Simon & Schuster Trade, 1996.

Janofsky, Michael. "Colorado Fuels U.S. Debate Over Use of Behavioral Drugs." *New York Times,* November 25, 1999.

Can ADD Occur with Other Disorders?

Dunne, J.E. "Attention-Deficit/Hyperactivity Disorder And Associated Childhood Disorders." *Primary Care* 26 (1999): 349-72.

Rohde, L.A. et al. "ADHD in a School Sample of Brazilian Adolescents: A Study of Prevalence, Comorbid Conditions, and Impairments." *Journal of the American Academy of Child and Adolescent Psychiatry* 38 (1999): 716-22.

Is There a Litmus Test for ADD?

Saltus, R. "Brain Scans Seen as Test in Attention Disorder." *Boston Globe,* December 17, 1999.

Does Everyone Who Moves Have ADD?

Bandura, A. "Behavioral Psychotherapy." *Scientific American* 216 (1967): 78-86.

Rutter, M. and D. Quinton. "Psychiatric Disorder: Ecological Factors and Concepts of Causation." In *Ecological Factors in Human Development,* edited by H. McGurk. Amsterdam, The Netherlands: *North-Holland Publishing Co.,* 1977.

Shaw, Daniel S. and Richard Q. Bell. "Developmental Theories of Parental Contributors to Antisocial Behavior." *Journal of Abnormal Child Psychology* 21 (1993): 493-518.

Does ADD Occur in Girls Too?

Arcia, Emily and C. Keith Conners. "Gender Differences in ADHD?" *Journal of Developmental & Behavioral Pediatrics* 19 (1998): 77-83.

Carlson, C.L., L. Tamm, M. Gaub. "Gender Differences in Children with ADHD, ODD, and Co-Occurring ADHD/ODD Identified in a School Population." *Journal of the American Academy of Child and Adolescent Psychiatry.* 36 (1997): 1706-14.

Robison, Linda M. et al. National Trends in the Prevalence of Attention-Deficit/Hyperactivity Disorder and the Prescribing of Methylphenidate among School-Age Children: 1990-1995. *Clinical Pediatrics* 38 (1999): 209-17.

SECTION II

How Does One Cope with ADD?

Barkley, Russell A. *ADHD: What Do We Know?* New York: Guilford Publications, 1992, video tape.

Barkley, Russell A. *Attention Deficit Hyperactivity Disorders: A Handbook for Diagnosis and Treatment.* New York: Guilford Publications, 1990.

Barocas, R., R. Seifer, Arnold J. Sameroff. "Defining Environmental Risk: Multiple Dimensions of Psychological Vulnerability." *American Journal of Community Psychology* 13 (1985): 433-47.

Beugin, M.E. *Coping with ADD.* Calgary, Alberta, Canada: Detselig Enterprises, 1990.

Children's Hospital of Philadelphia Staff. *A Parents' Guide to Attention Deficit Disorders.* New York: Dell Publishing Co., 1991.

Garber, Stephen W. et al. *If Your Child Is Hyperactive, Inattentive, Impulsive, Distractible: Helping the ADD (Attention Deficit Disoder)-Hyperactive Child.* New York: Random House, 1990.

Garfinkel, B. and D. Cantwell. *ADHD Active Partnerships.* Salt Lake City, UT: Neurology, Learning & Behavior Center, 1990, video tape.

Gordon, Michael. *ADHD-Hyperactivity: A Consumer's Guide for Parents and Teachers.* DeWitt, NY: GSI Publications, 1990.

Greenberg, Gregory S. and Wade F. Horn. *Attention Deficit Hyperactivity Disorder: Questions and Answers for Parents.* Champaign, IL: Research Press, 1991.

Harris, Judith Rich. *The Nurture Assumption: Why Children Turn Out the Way They Do: Parents Matter Less Than You Think and Peers Matter More.* New York: Simon & Schuster Trade, 1998.

Hartmann, Thom. *Attention Deficit Disorder: A Different Perception.* Lancaster, PA: Underwood/Miller, 1993.

Ingersoll, Barbara D. *Your Hyperactive Child: A Parent's Guide to Coping with Attention Deficit Disorder.* New York: Doubleday & Co., 1988.

Parker, Harvey C. *The ADD Hyperactivity Workbook for Parents, Teachers and Kids.* Plantation, FL: Specialty Press, 1988.

Sameroff, Arnold J. *Models of Developmental Risk in Handbook of Infant Mental Health.* Edited by Charles H. Zeanah, Jr. New York: Guilford Publications, 1993.

Silver, Larry. *The Misunderstood Child: Understanding and Coping with Your Child's Learning Disabilities.* 3rd ed. New York: Random House, 1998.

How Does One Care for a Child with ADD?

Abikoff, Howard et al. "The Effects of Auditory Stimulation on the Arithmetic Performance of Children with ADHD and Nondisabled Children." *Journal of Learning Diasbilities* 29 (1996): 238-46.

Braswell, Lauren and Michael Bloomquist. *Cognitive-Behavorial Therapy with ADHD Children: Child, Family and School Interventions.* New York: Guilford Publications, 1991.

Buck, Pearl S. *The Joy of Children.* New York: The John Day Company, 1964.

Diller, Lawrence H. *Running on Ritalin: A Physician Reflects on Children, Society, and Performance in a Pill.* New York: Bantam Books, 1998.

Goldstein, Sam and Michael Goldstein. *Managing Attention Disorders in Children: A Guide for Practitioners.* Somerset, NJ: Wiley Interscience Press, 1990.

Gordon, Thomas. *Parent Effectiveness Training: The Tested New Way to Raise Responsible Children.* New York: David McKay Co., 1970.

Gould, M.A. *Psychological Symptoms: A Consumer's Guide to Diagnosis and Available Treatments.* New York: Berkley Publishing, 1990.

Hafner, Claire. *Learning to Parent a Hyperactive Child.* Wilmington, DE: GP King Publications, 1987.

Howard, B. J. "Discipline in Early Childhood." *Pediatric Clinics of North America* 38 (1991): 1351-69.

Meeks, Carolyn Ann and Michael J. Buschmohle. *Prescriptions for Parenting.* New York: Little, Brown, 1990.

Robin, Arthur L. and Sharon L. Foster. *Negotiating Parent-Adolescent Conflict: A Behavioral-Family Systems Approach.* New York: Guilford Publications, 1989.

Turecki, Stanley. *Normal Children Have Problems, Too: How Parents Can Understand and Help.* New York: Bantam Books, 1994.

Vinson, D.C. "Therapy for Attention Deficit Hyperactivity Disorder." *Archives of Family Medicine* 35 (1994): 445-51.

Is There an Antibiotic for ADD?

Cantwell, Dennis P., James Swanson, Daniel F. Connor. "Case Study: Adverse Response to Clonidine." *Journal of the American Academy of Child and Adolescent Psychiatry* 36 (1997): 539-44.

Copeland, Edna. *Medications for Attention Disorders and Related Medical Problems.* Atlanta: 3 C's of Childhood, 1991.

Dunnick, J.K. and J.R. Hailey. "Experimental Studies on the Long-Term Effects of Methylphenidate Hydrochloride." *Toxicology* 30 (1995): 77-84.

Fine, S. and C. Johnston. "Drug and Placebo Side Effects in Methylphenidate-Placebo Trial for Attention Deficit Hyperactivity Disorder." *Child Psychiatry and Human Development* 24 (1993): 25-30.

Greenhill, L.L. and Osman, B.B. *Ritalin: Theory and Patient Management.* Larchmont, NY: Mary Ann Leibert Inc., 1991.

Gualtieri, C.T. et al. "Tardive Dyskinesia and Other Movement Disorders in Children Treated with Psychotropic Drugs." *Journal of the American Academy of Child Psychiatry* 19 (1980): 491-510.

Gupta, Vidya B. *Manual of Developmental and Behavioral Problems in Children*, vol. 9 of *Pediatric Habilitation Series.* New York: Marcel Dekker, 1998.

Henderson, T.A. and V.W. Fischer. "Effects of Methylphenidate (Ritalin) on Mammalian Myocardial Ultrastructure." *American Journal of Cardiovascular Pathology* 5 (1995): 68-78.

Hunt, R.D., A.F. Arnsten, M.D. Asbell. "An Open Trial of Guanfacine in the Treatment of Attention-Deficit Hyperactivity Disorder." *Journal of the American Academy of Child and Adolescent Psychiatry* 34 (1995): 50-4.

Law, S.F. and R.J. Schachar. "Do Typical Clinical Doses of Methylphenidate Cause Tics in Children Treated for Attention-Deficit Hyperactivity Disorder?" *Journal of the American Academy of Child and Adolescent Psychiatry* 38 (1999): 944-51.

MTA Cooperative Group. "A 14-Month Randomized Clinical Trial of Treatment Strategies for Attention-Deficit/Hyperactivity Disorder." *Archives of General Psychiatry.* 56 (1999): 1073-86.

Musten, L.M. et al. "Effects of Methylphenidate on Preschool Children with ADHD: Cognitive and Behavioral Functions." *Journal of the American Academy of Child and Adolescent Psychiatry* 36 (1997): 1407-15.

Noble, Holcomb B. "Study Backs a Drug for Hyperactive Children." *New York Times*, December 15, 1999.

Will My Child Get Addicted to Ritalin?
Cooper, James R. et al. "Prescription Drug Diversion Control and Medical Practice." *JAMA* 268 (1992): 1306-10.

Fulton, A.I. and W.R. Yates. "Family Abuse of Methylphenidate." *American Family Physician* 38 (1988): 143-5.

Lambert, N.M. "Adolescent Outcomes for Hyperactive Children: Perspectives on General and Specific Patterns of Childhood Risk for Adolescent Educational, Social, and Mental Health Problems." *American Psychologist* 43 (1988): 786-99.

Loney, Jan. "Substance Abuse in Adolescents: Diagnostic Issues Derived from Studies of Attention Deficit Disorder with Hyperactivity." *NIDA Research Monograph* 77 (1988): 19-26.

Massello, W. III and D.A. Carpenter. "A Fatality Due to the Intranasal Abuse of Methylphenidate (Ritalin)." *Journal of Forensic Science* 44 (1999): 220-1.

Volkow, Nora D. et al. "Dopamine Transporter Occupancies in the Human Brain Induced by Therapeutic Doses of Oral Methylphenidate." *American Journal of Psychiatry* 155 (1998): 1325-31.

Volkow, Nora D. et al. "Is Methylphenidate Like Cocaine? Studies on Their Pharmacokinetics and Distribution in the Human Brain." *Archives of General Psychiatry* 52 (1995): 456-63.

Wilens, T.E., J. Biederman, E. Mick. "Does ADHD Affect the Course of Substance Abuse? Findings from a Sample of Adults With and Without ADHD." *American Journal of Addiction* 7 (1998): 156-63.

Is ADD Caused by Sugar, Dyes, or Salicylates?

Aman, M.G., E.A. Mitchell, S.H. Turbott. "The Effects of Essential Fatty Acid Supplementation by Efamol in Hyperactive Children." *Journal of Abnormal Child Psychology* 15 (1987): 75-90.

Arnold, L.E. et al. "Gamma-Linolenic Acid for Attention-Deficit Hyperactivity Disorder: Placebo-Controlled Comparison to D-Amphetamine." *Biological Psychiatry* 25 (1989): 222-8.

Behar, D. et al. "Sugar Challenge Testing With Children Considered Behaviorally Asugar Reactive." *Nutrition and Behavior* 1 (1984): 277-88.

Biederman, Joseph et al. "Associations Between Childhood Asthma and ADHD: Issues of Psychiatric Comorbidity and Familiarity." *Journal of the American Academy of Child and Adolescent Psychiatry* 33 (1994): 842-8.

Block, Mary A. *No More Ritalin.* New York: Kensington Publishing, 1996.

Boris, M. and F.S. Mandel. "Foods and Additives Are Common Causes of the Attention Deficit Hyperactive Disorder in Children." *Annals of Allergy* 72 (1994): 462-8.

Brody, Jane E. "Diet Change May Avert Need for Ritalin." *New York Times*, November 2, 1999.

Conners, C. Keith. *Feeding the Brain: How Foods Affect Children.* New York: Plenum Publishing, 1989.

DiBattista, D. and Mari-Lynn Shephard. "Primary School Teachers' Beliefs and Advice to Parents Concerning Sugar Consumption and Activity in Children." *Psychological Reports* 72 (1993): 47-55.

Egger, E. et al. "Controlled Trial of Oligoantigenic Treatment in the Hyperkinetic Syndrome." *Lancet* 1 (1985): 540-5.

Feingold, Ben F. *Why Your Child is Hyperactive.* New York: Random House, 1975.

Kruesi, M.J.P. et al. "Effects of Sugar and Aspartame on Aggression and Activity in Children." *American Journal of Psychiatry* 144 (1987): 1487-90.

McGee, R., W. Stanton, M. Sears. "Allergic Disorders and Attention Deficit Disorder in Children." *Journal of Abnormal Child Psychology* 21 (1993): 79-88.

Mitchell, E.A. et al. "Clinical Characteristics and Serum Essential Fatty Acid Levels in Hyperactive Children." *Clinical Pediatrics* 26 (1987): 406-11.

Perry, Christine A. et al. "Health Effects of Salicylates in Foods and Drugs." *Nutrition Reviews* 54 (1996): 225-40.

Robinson, J. and A. Ferguson. "Food Sensitivity and the Nervous System: Hyperactivity, Addiction and Criminal Behavior." *Nutrition Research Reviews* 5 (1992): 203-23.

Roshon, M.S. and R.L. Hagen. "Sugar Consumption, Locomotion, Task Orientation, and Learning in Preschool Children." *Journal of Abnormal Child Psychology* 17 (1989): 349-57.

Sculte-Koerne, G. et al. "Effect of an oligoantigenic diet on the behavior of hyperkinetic children." *Zeitschrift fur Kinder und Jugendpsychiatrie* 24 (1996): 176-83.

Stevens, Laura J. et al. "Essential Fatty Acid Metabolism in Boys With Attention-Deficit Hyperactivity Disorder." *American Journal of Clinical Nutrition* 62 (1995): 761-8.

Weiss, B. et al. "Behavioral Responses to Artificial Food Colors." *Science* 207 (1980): 1487-8.

Wender, E.H. "Review of Research on Relationship of Nutritive Sweeteners and Behavior." In *Diet and Behavior, a Series of Regional Forums.* Boston: The Sugar Association, 1991.

Wolraich, Mark L., D.B. Wilson, J.W. Whie. "The Effect of Sugar on Behavior or Cognition in Children: A Meta-analysis." *JAMA* 274 (1995): 1617-21.

Do Children Outgrow ADD?

Weiss, Gabrielle and Lily T. Hechtman. *Hyperactive Children Grown Up: Empirical Findings and Theoretical Considerations.* New York: Guilford Publications, 1986.

Wender, Paul. *The Hyperactive Child, Adolescent and Adult.* New York: Oxford University Press, 1987.

Is Everything Lost in ADD?

Armstrong, Thomas. *The Myth of the ADD Child: 50 Ways to Improve Your Child's Behavior and Attention Span Without Drugs, Labels, or Coercion.* New York: NAL/Dutton, 1995.

Handly, Robert, Jane Handly, Pauline Neff. *The Life*plus Program for Getting Unstuck.* New York: Rawson Associates, 1989.

Hartmann, Thom. *Attention Deficit Disorder: A Different Perspective.* Grass Valley, CA: Underwood Books, 1993.

What About Alternative Treatments for ADD?

Anonymous. "Megavitamins and the Hyperactive Child." *Nutrition Reviews* 43(1985): 105-7.

Balch, James F. and Phyllis Balch. *Prescriptions for Nutritional Healing: A Practical A-Z Reference to Drug-Free Remedies Using Vitamins, Herbs and Food Supplements.* 2nd ed. Garden City Park, NY: Avery Publishing Group, 1997.

Balon, Jeffrey et al. "A Comparison of Active and Simulated Chiropractic Manipulation as Adjunctive Treatment for Childhood Asthma." *New England Journal of Medicine* 339 (1998): 1013-20.

Crook, William G. *The Yeast Connection: A Medical Breakthrough.* New York: Random House, 1986.

Denkowski, K.M. and G.C. Denkowski. "Is Group Progressive Relaxation Training as Effective with Hyperactive Children as Individual EMG Biofeedback Treatment?" *Biofeedback and Self-Regulation* 9 (1984): 353-64.

Felder, Michael et al. "Spinal Manipulation for Tension-type Headache." Discussion. *JAMA* 282 (1999): 231-2.

Ferraro, S. "Brain Boon? An In-depth Look at Serotonin and a Controversial Nutritional Supplement." *Daily News* (New York), September 28, 1998.

Garattini, Silvio. "Pharmacocentricity: From Elixirs to Magic Bullets." Supplement IV. *Lancet* 354 (1999), 51.

Haslam, R.H. "Is There a Role for Megavitamin Therapy in the Treatment of Attention Deficit Hyperactivity Disorder?" *Advances in Neurology* 58 (1992): 303-10.

Iovino, I. et al. "Colored Overlays for Visual Perceptual Deficits in Children With Reading Disability and Attention Deficit/Hyperactivity Disorder: Are They Differentially Effective?" *Journal of Clinical and Experimental Neuropsychology* 20 (1998): 791-806.

Kozielec, T. and B. Starobrat-Hermelin. "Assessment of Magnesium Levels in Children with Attention Deficit Hyperactivity Disorder (ADHD)." *Magnesium Research* 10 (1997): 143-8.

Kemper, Kathi J. *The Holistic Pediatrician: A Parent's Comprehensive Guide to Safe and Effective Therapies for the 25 Most Common Childhood Ailments.* New York: HarperCollins Publications, 1996.

Lee, S.W. "Biofeedback as a Treatment For Childhood Hyperactivity: A Critical Review of the Literature." *Psychological Reports* 68 (1991): 163-92.

McConnell, H. "Catecholamine Metabolism in the Attention Deficit Disorder: Implications for the Use of Amino Acid Precursor Therapy." *Medical Hypotheses* 17 (1985): 305-11.

Nemzer, E. et al. "Amino Acid Supplementation as Therapy for Attention Deficit Disorder." *Journal of the American Academy of Child and Adolescent Psychiatry*, 25 (1986): 509-13.

Raymer, R. and R. Poppen. "Behavioral Relaxation Training with Hyperactive Children." *Journal of Behavior Therapy and Experimental Psychiatry* 16 (1985): 309-16.

Rimland, B. "Megavitamins and Hyperactivity." Letter to the Editor. *Pediatrics* 78 (1986): 374-5.

Shekelle, Paul G. "What Role for Chiropractic in Health Care?" Editorial. *New England Journal of Medicine* 339 (1998): 1074-5.

Zieffle, T.H. and D.M. Romney. "Comparison of Self-Instruction and Relaxation Training in Reducing Impulsive and Inattentive Behavior of Learning Disabled Children on Cognitive Tasks." *Psychological Reports* 57 (1985): 271-4.

Is Alternative Medicine Fact or Fiction?

Bigby, Michael. "Snake Oil for the 21st Century." *Archives of Dermatology* 134 (1998): 1512-4.

Breggin, Peter R. *Talking Back to Ritalin: What Doctors Aren't Telling You About Stimulants for Children.* Monroe, ME: Common Courage Press, 1998.

Breggin, Peter R. *Toxic Psychiatry: Why Therapy, Empathy, and Love Must Replace the Drugs, Electroshock, and Biochemical Theories of the 'New Psychiatry.'* New York: St. Martin's Press, 1994.

Giere, Ronald N. *Understanding Scientific Reasoning.* 4th ed. Fort Worth, TX: Harcourt Brace College Publications, 1996.

Golden, G.S. "Symposium on Learning Disorders: Controversial Therapies." *Pediatric Clinics of North America* 31 (1984): 459-69.

Stein, David B. and Peter R. Breggin. *Ritalin Is Not the Answer : A Drug-Free, Practical Program for Children Diagnosed With ADD or ADHD.* San Francisco: Jossey-Bass Publishers; 1999.

Young, James Harvey. *American Health Quackery: Collected Essays.* Princeton, NJ: Princeton University Press, 1992.

Resource Section

ORGANIZATIONS

Children and Adults with Attention Deficit Disorder (CHADD)
8181 Professional Plaza
Suite 201
Landover, Maryland 20785
Telephone: (800) 233-4050
Web site: www.chadd.org

National Attention Deficit Disorder Association (NADDA)
1788 Second Street
Suite 200
Highland Park, Illinois 60035
Telephone: (847) 432-ADDA (2332)
Web site: www.add.org

Learning Disabilities Association (LDA)
4156 Library Road
Pittsburgh, Pennsylvania 15234-1349
Telephone: (412) 341-1515
Web site: www.ldanatl.org

PUBLICATIONS

Explaining About ADD to Kids (Readings for Children)

Dixon, Emily and Kathleen Nadeau. *Learning to Slow Down and Pay Attention.* Washington, DC: Magination Press, 1997.

Gehret, Jeanne. *Eagle Eyes: A Child's Guide to Paying Attention.* Fairport, NY: Verbal Images Press, 1991.

Goldstein, Sam and Michael Goldstein. *It's Just Attention Disorder.* Salt Lake City, UT: Neurology, Learning and Behavior Center; telephone order: (801) 532-1482; video tape with manual.

Gordon, Michael. *Jumpin' Johnny, Get Back to Work! A Child's Guide to ADHD-Hyperactivity.* DeWitt, NY: GSI Publications, 1991.

Gordon, Michael. *I Would If I Could: A Teenager's Guide to ADHD-Hyperactivity.* DeWitt, NY: GSI Publications, 1993.

Moss, Deborah. *Shelly the Hyperactive Turtle.* Bethesda, MD: Woodbine House, 1989.

Parker, Roberta N. and Harvey Parker. *Making the Grade: An Adolescent's Struggle with ADD.* Plantation, FL: Specialty Press, 1992.

School and ADD

Copeland, Edna D. *Attention Disorders: The School's Vital Role.* Atlanta, GA: 3 C's of Childhood, 1989, video tape.

Fowler, Mary Cahill. *Educator's Manual.* Overland, MD: CHADD, 1992

Goldstein, Sam. *Educating Inattentive Children.* Salt Lake City, UT: Neurology, Learning and Behavior Center, 1989, video.

Hallahan, D.P. and J.M. Kauffman. *Exceptional Children: Introduction to Special Education.* Englewood Cliffs, NY: Prentice Hall, 1988.

Levine, Melvin D. *Keeping A Head in School: A Student's Book About Learning Disabilities and Learning Disorders.* Rev. ed. Cambridge, MA: Educators Publishing Service, 1990.

Parker, Harvey C. *ADAPT: Attention Deficit Accommodation Plan for Teaching—Student Planbook.* Plantation, FL: Specialty Press, Florida, 1992.

Parker, Harvey C. *ADAPT: Attention Deficit Accommodation Plan for Teaching: Teacher's Planbook.* Plantation, FL: Specialty Press, Florida, 1992.

Parker, Harvey C. *The ADD Hyperactivity Handbook for Schools: Effective Strategies for Identifying and Teaching ADD Students in Elementary and Secondary Schools.* Plantation, FL: Specialty Press, 1998.

WEB SITES

American Academy of Child and Adolescent Psychiatry
www.aacap.org/publications/factsfam/noattent.htm
This site gives information in simple language about attention deficit disorder.

ADD Action Group
www.addgroup.org
A non-profit organization that focuses on attention deficit disorder, learning disability, dyslexia, and autism.

Children and Adults with Attention Deficit Disorder (CHADD)
www.chadd.org
CHADD works to improve the lives of people with attention-deficit/hyperactivity disorder through education, advocacy, and support.

WEB SITES (continued)

CHADD-Canada, Inc.
www.members.tripod.com/~chaddcanada/index.html
A non-profit parent-run organization that aims to help support, educate, and ultimatly better the lives of individuals with ADD and of those
who care for them.

Learning Disabilities Association of America (LDA)
www.ldanatl.org
A national, non-profit organization for advancing the education and general welfare of children and adults of normal or potentially normal intelligence who manifest disabilities of a perceptual, conceptual, or coordinative nature.

National Attention Deficit Disorder Association (NADDA)
www.ADD.org
NADDA's mission is to help people with ADD lead happier, more successful lives, through education, research, and public advocacy.

National Institutes of Health (NIH)
www.nimh.nih.gov/publicat/adhd.cfm
This extension to the basic NIH Web site (www.nimh.nih.gov) takes you directly to NIH publication number 96-3572, written for the general public and focusing directly on attention deficit disorder.

Index

ABOUT THE AUTHOR

Dr. Vidya Bhushan Gupta is Chief of Developmental Pediatrics, Department of Pediatrics, Metropolitan Hospital Center, New York, New York. He is also Associate Professor of Clinical Pediatrics at the New York Medical College and a visiting associate research scientist at the Gertrude H. Sergievsky Center, College of Physicians and Surgeons, Columbia University, New York.

Certified by the American Board of Pediatrics in 1987, Dr. Gupta is a fellow of the American Academy of Pediatrics. He serves on the Project Advisory Committee of the Medical Home Initiatives for Children With Special Health Care Needs of the American Academy of Pediatrics, and is also a member of the Society for Developmental Pediatrics and of the Society for Developmental and Behavioral Pediatrics.

The author of *Manual of Developmental and Behavioral Problems in Children*, Dr. Gupta's scholarly articles have appeared in such publications as *Pediatrics*, the *American Journal of Clinical Epidemiology*, *Indian Pediatrics*, *The Record*, and *Weber Studies*.

Dr. Gupta received an M.B.B.S. degree and an M.D. degree in Pediatrics from Maulana Azad Medical College, University of Delhi, New Delhi, India. He also holds an M.P.H. degree from Columbia University School of Public Health, New York, New York.